S0-ADD-995

WORLD HISTORY

The French Revolution

Don Nardo

LUCENT BOOKS
A part of Gale, Cengage Learning

Property of
Bradley Beach Public Library

GALE
CENGAGE Learning

Detroit • New York • San Francisco • New Haven, Conn • Waterville, Maine • London

© 2008 Gale, Cengage Learning

ALL RIGHTS RESERVED. No part of this work covered by the copyright hereon may be reproduced, transmitted, stored, or used in any form or by any means graphic, electronic, or mechanical, including but not limited to photocopying, recording, scanning, digitizing, taping, Web distribution, information networks, or information storage and retrieval systems, except as permitted under Section 107 or 108 of the 1976 United States Copyright Act, without the prior written permission of the publisher.

Every effort has been made to trace the owners of copyrighted material.

LIBRARY OF CONGRESS CATALOGING-IN-PUBLICATION DATA

Nardo, Don.
  The French Revolution / by Don Nardo.
      p. cm. — (World history)
  Includes bibliographical references and index.
  ISBN 978-1-4205-0098-1 (hardcover)
  1. France—History—Revolution, 1789–1799--Juvenile literature. I. Title.
  DC148.N267 2008
  944.04--dc22   2008007968

Lucent Books
27500 Drake Rd.
Farmington Hills, MI 48331

ISBN-13: 978-1-4205-0098-1
ISBN-10: 1-4205-0098-8

Printed in the United States of America
1 2 3 4 5 6 7 12 11 10 09 08

Contents

Foreword

Each year, on the first day of school, nearly every history teacher faces the task of explaining why his or her students should study history. Many reasons have been given. One is that lessons exist in the past from which contemporary society can benefit and learn. Another is that exploration of the past allows us to see the origins of our customs, ideas, and institutions. Concepts such as democracy, ethnic conflict, or even things as trivial as fashion or mores, have historical roots.

Reasons such as these impress few students, however. If anything, these explanations seem remote and dull to young minds. Yet history is anything but dull. And therein lies what is perhaps the most compelling reason for studying history: History is filled with great stories. The classic themes of literature and drama—love and sacrifice, hatred and revenge, injustice and betrayal, adversity and overcoming adversity—fill the pages of history books, feeding the imagination as well as any of the great works of fiction do.

The story of the Children's Crusade, for example, is one of the most tragic in history. In 1212 Crusader fever hit Europe. A call went out from the pope that all good Christians should journey to Jerusalem to drive out the hated Muslims and return the city to Christian control. Heeding the call, thousands of children made the journey. Parents bravely allowed many children to go, and entire communities were inspired by the faith of these small Crusaders. Unfortunately, many boarded ships captained by slave traders, who enthusiastically sold the children into slavery as soon as they arrived at their destination. Thousands died from disease, exposure, and starvation on the long march across Europe to the Mediterranean Sea. Others perished at sea.

Another story, from a modern and more familiar place, offers a soul-wrenching view of personal humiliation but also the ability to rise above it. Hatsuye Egami was one of 110,000 Japanese Americans sent to internment camps during World War II. "Since yesterday we Japanese have ceased to be human beings," he wrote in his diary. "We are numbers. We are no longer Egamis, but the number 23324. A tag with that number is on every trunk, suitcase and bag. Tags, also, on our breasts." Despite such dehumanizing treatment, most internees worked hard to control their bitterness. They created workable communities inside the camps and demonstrated again and again their loyalty as Americans.

These are but two of the many stories from history that can be found in the pages of the Lucent Books World History series. All World History titles rely on sound research and verifiable evidence, and all give students a clear sense of time, place, and chronology through maps and timelines as well as text.

All titles include a wide range of authoritative perspectives that demonstrate the complexity of historical interpretation and sharpen the reader's critical thinking skills. Formally documented quotations and annotated bibliographies enable students to locate and evaluate sources, often instantaneously via the Internet, and serve as valuable tools for further research and debate.

Finally, Lucent's World History titles present rousing good stories, featuring vivid primary source quotations drawn from unique, sometimes obscure sources such as diaries, public records, and contemporary chronicles. In this way, the voices of participants and witnesses as well as important biographers and historians bring the study of history to life. As we are caught up in the lives of others, we are reminded that we too are characters in the ongoing human saga, and we are better prepared for our own roles.

1756–1763
France and its allies fight Britain and its allies in the Seven Years War; France loses.

1787
France's chief financial minister tells King Louis that the country's tax system must be reformed; the U.S. Constitution is drafted.

July 14, 1789
A Paris mob storms and captures the fortress-prison known as the Bastille.

August 4, 1789
The National Assembly abolishes the nobility's feudal privileges.

1774
Louis XVI and Marie-Antoinette become king and queen of France.

A.D. 1700   1780   1789

1776
Britain's thirteen American colonies declare their independence and become the United States.

1781
With French military assistance, the Americans defeat the British at Yorktown, winning the Revolutionary War.

June 17, 1789
The delegates of France's Third Estate declare themselves to be the country's National Assembly.

August 27, 1789
The Assembly adopts the Declaration of the Rights of Man and the Citizen.

1778
Two of the great Enlightenment thinkers, Voltaire Rousseau (pictured), die.

the French Revolution

1791
The great Austrian composer Wolfgang Mozart dies; in France, King Louis tries but fails to escape to Germany.

1792
France declares war on Austria.

1794
Robespierre, chief architect of the Reign of Terror, is executed.

1799
Napoléon seizes power in France and declares that the French Revolution is over.

1790   **1795**   **1800**

January 21, 1793
King Louis is publicly beheaded.

October 16, 1793
Marie-Antoinette is executed.

1795
The Directory, a government headed by a five-man council, takes charge of France.

1797
French general Napoléon Bonaparte concludes a peace treaty with Austria.

1798
English doctor Edward Jenner discovers the vaccination for smallpox; Napoléon invades Egypt.

The Cradle of the Modern World

Each decade that passes, a number of political, military, social, and/or natural events occur that affect the affairs of a city, people, nation, or even a continent for years to come. New nations declare their independence; popular or unpopular leaders come to power or die; battles are won or lost; social protests force new, more progressive laws to be enacted; famines, epidemics, volcanic eruptions, and other natural disasters destroy cities and devastate local populations; and so on.

Only rarely does a single event in one country significantly or radically change the course of history across almost the entire world for generations to come. Three such events in the past century were the 1929 stock market crash, which initiated a devastating global economic depression; Nazi Germany's invasion of Poland in 1939, which sparked World War II, the largest and most costly war in history; and the 9/11 attacks in New York City in 2001, which set in motion the so-called global war on terror.

Radical Political Change

The French Revolution, which began in 1789, was every bit as momentous as the above-mentioned events; and its consequences and influences were almost certainly even more profound and long-lasting. "This great drama transformed the whole meaning of political change," noted historian William Doyle points out, "and the contemporary [today's] world would be inconceivable if it had not happened."[1]

Doyle emphasizes "political change" when describing the Revolution for good reason. Most earlier revolutions in world history did not drastically alter the political status quo. Thousands of people might die and entire cities might be looted or burned. But in nearly all cases, the leaders who took charge in the end ruled in the same manner, utilizing the same political systems, as those they had overthrown. With only a tiny handful of exceptions, these systems were monarchies in one form or another. That is, a king, queen, emperor, or some other absolute monarch was in charge. And usually his or her word was law.

What made the French Revolution so different was that it completely scrapped and swept aside France's age-old monarchy. Even the American Revolution, another major historical turning point that occurred a little more than a decade earlier, had not gone that far. True, the American rebels had shaken off British rule and set up their own nation, the United States, with a progressive political system in which the people elect their leaders. But the Americans did not, in the process, topple and eradicate

An illustration of a meeting held by delegates during the French Revolution, one of the most momentous events to impact the world.

Britain's monarchy and execute thousands of its aristocrats.

In contrast, this is exactly what happened in France. Between 1789 and 1794, the French people dethroned and arrested their king, Louis XVI, dismantled his monarchy, and executed him, his wife, and thousands of other nobles. The revolutionaries replaced these leaders with a new system based on the then radical concepts of popular rule, personal liberty, and equal justice for all.

After that, France was never the same. Since that time, its people and its government have periodically undergone turmoil and wrestled with how best to serve the interests of the country and its population. But always, the ideals of the Revolution—liberty, equality, and fraternity (brotherhood)—have remained sacred and fundamental. And the French celebrate their independence day (July 14, when a French mob captured the monarchy's prison-fortress, the Bastille) with just as much pride and pomp as the Americans celebrate July 4.

An Historical Tidal Wave

Even more momentous, however, was the impact the French Revolution had on its European neighbors and eventually the rest of the globe. At the time the Revolution broke out, France was one

The destruction of France's monarchy was not only significant for France, but also for its European neighbors.

of the three or four leading world powers. Its affairs and the aspirations of its leaders had long been intimately intertwined with those of other nations. Therefore, the destruction of France's monarchy and the other turmoil the Revolution wrought inevitably sent shock waves throughout Europe and well beyond. As the noted modern scholar Jacques Solé puts it, "attitudes toward history and social order could no longer be the same after 1799 [the year the Revolution officially ended] as they had been before 1789. An ideological tidal wave, the French Revolution was, in this sense, the cradle of the modern world. Its long-range influence was to prove more important in this respect than in its immediate effects."[2]

Indeed, partly inspired by France's great rebellion, many other political revolutions and reform movements swept Europe and the Americas in the nineteenth century. These forever changed the attitudes of the peoples involved about how they should be ruled and helped to set the stage for the remarkable spread of democracy in the twentieth century. "The shadow of the Revolution fell across the whole of the nineteenth century and beyond," Doyle writes. "Until 1917 [when the Russian Revolution began] few would have disputed that [the French Revolution] was the greatest revolution in the history of the world; and even after that its claims to primacy remain strong. It was the first modern revolution, the archetypical one [i.e., the model]. After it, nothing in the European world remained the same, and we are all heirs to its influence."[3]

Chapter One

The Revolution's Complex Roots

For the sake of convenience, historians and other writers routinely refer to the French Revolution as a historical "event." In reality, however, it was not a single event, but rather, as William Doyle terms it, "a series of developments, bewildering to most contemporaries, which stretched over a number of years."[4] Indeed, after its outbreak in 1789, the Revolution underwent several distinct phases, each with its own set of leaders, goals, and outcomes in the ten years that followed.

Similarly, it is fruitless to search for a single or simple cause for this great watershed in human history. It had multiple roots, some of which were complex and built up over the course of generations. A number of the Revolution's causes were economic in nature. Others were social and political, while still others involved the emergence of new ideas about human equality and justice.

That these diverse causes came together and ignited enormous upheaval in France rather than somewhere else in that era is perhaps not surprising. First, with almost 27 million people, the nation was by far the most populous in Europe and indeed in the world. (Germany and Italy had about 18.5 million each; the then combined Belgium and Luxembourg, 18 million; Great Britain and Ireland, roughly 16 million; and Spain, about 10.5 million.) Thus, the French government had more people to keep track of, protect, appease, and control than did the governments of its neighbors. And if its capacity to appease and control were to waver, it had more to lose.

France was also one of the world's most powerful and ambitious countries. It had an elaborate monarchy, many entrenched aristocratic institutions, a large army and navy, and numerous foreign colonies and commitments. All of these things were enormously costly to maintain. Also any inability to continue paying for them was bound to lead to instability or worse.

Moreover, with its large population, power, and prestige on the world stage, France was a major center of learning, intellectual debate, and new, and in some cases radical, ideas. "Because there was more wealth [and] more [intellectual] enlightenment in France," says historian Arthur J. May, "Frenchmen were more dynamically discontented with the status quo, more ready for drastic changes."[5]

France's Economic Woes

Thus, though revolution was not inevitable in eighteenth-century France, it was distinctly feasible. All that was needed was some major setback to touch off a chain of events that could potentially threaten the stability of its existing social and political order. One such setback—a huge one—was a conflict fought from 1756 to 1763. In the Seven Years War, France formed an alliance with Russia, Austria, and Sweden and clashed with the combined forces of Britain and Prussia (Germany). The outcome was disastrous for France. Its land armies were routed by those of Prussia, and the British navy defeated French fleets on the high seas. Britain also pushed France out of India and North America (where the conflict was called the French and Indian War), except for some Caribbean islands where French colonies survived but suffered serious economic reversals. (As a result, Britain emerged as the world's dominant colonial power.)

These losses left France not only beaten and humiliated but also financially

The Seven Years War

The Seven Years War, fought from 1756 to 1763, is sometimes referred to as the first true "world war" because it involved all the major European powers of that day, plus their colonies around the globe. The conflict erupted partly over who should rule in Austria and elsewhere in Europe. It was also a struggle between the British and French empires over colonial possessions. One of the opposing alliances consisted mainly of Britain and Prussia; the other consisted of France, Austria, Russia, and Sweden. Somewhere between 900,000 and 1.4 million people died, and hundreds of thousands were wounded in this disastrous war. The biggest loser in the end was France, which forfeited most of its overseas empire, thereby weakening the authority and image of the French monarchy.

strapped. The French government had borrowed heavily to finance the war, and now it was unclear how it was going to pay its gigantic debts. Just making the regular payments on them used up more than half of the nation's tax revenues in the years immediately following the war. Making matters worse, French tax revenues were mostly below normal levels in the mid-1780s.

Incredibly, even in the face of these economic woes, in the 1770s the French government again borrowed money to wage war. The new king, Louis XVI, who had succeeded his grandfather, Louis XV, on the throne in 1774, agreed to aid the Americans in their bid for independence from the British. Hoping to humble its archenemy, Britain, as well as regain some influence in North America, France sent ships and soldiers. These were instrumental in the American victory and the survival of the infant United States. However, though it gained prestige in the affair, France made no territorial gains and only fell further into debt.

The economic situation was dire, therefore, when the bright and practical Charles Alexandre de Calonne became

The British seize Quebec from France during the Seven Years War.

Should All French Share the Burden?

In a speech delivered in February 1787, King Louis's financial minister, Charles Alexandre de Calonne, advocated the principal of "uniformity" in taxation, that is, the idea that all French, regardless of social rank, should share the tax burden.

His Majesty has first of all considered the various forms of administration which occur in those provinces without [local] Estates. In order that the distribution of taxation may cease to be unequal and arbitrary, he has decided to confide the task to the landowners and he has derived from the first principles of the monarchy the general plan of a graduated series of deliberative assemblies whereby the expression of the taxpayers' wishes and their observations on everything which concerns them will be transmitted from parish to district assemblies, thence to provincial assemblies and through them to the throne. Next His Majesty brought all his personal attention to bear on establishing the same principle of uniformity . . . in the distribution of the land tax . . . by restoring the original intention behind the tax, and by raising it to its true value without increasing anyone's contribution (indeed granting some relief to the people).

Quoted in "Calonne, 'Programs of Reform,' Address to the Assembly of Notables (1787)," Liberty, Equality, Fraternity: Exploring the French Revolution (http://chnm.gmu.edu/revolution/d/258/).

Before the French Revolution, Charles Alexandre de Calonne proposed a radical plan to overhaul France's economy.

France's chief finance minister in 1783. Calonne eventually concluded that business as usual could not continue, because the existing system was broken. There was no national budget and little central financial planning. Large sums of money ended up in the hands of diverse high-ranking officials who answered mostly to themselves. Moreover, the French people were already badly overtaxed, closing that avenue to raising extra revenue. Calonne told the king, "it is impossible to tax further, ruinous to be always borrowing, and not enough to confine ourselves to economic reforms. . . . With matters as they are . . . the only effective remedy, the only course left to take, the only means of managing finally to put the finances truly in order, must consist in revivifying [reorganizing] the entire state."[6]

Calonne proposed nothing less than radically reforming most state institutions, government ministries, and the national tax system, making all of them more efficient. The result, he argued, would be the production of far less waste and far more government income. In February 1787 Louis convened a meeting of the most powerful national officials and aristocrats to consider Calonne's proposals. But these men, the leaders of the entrenched social-political order known as the *ancien régime*, were selfish and lacked vision. Fearing they would lose some or all of their power and wealth if the system changed, they sought to destroy the plan. And Louis lacked the will and fortitude to counter them.

This put France in a difficult, potentially dangerous situation. As one scholar points out, the country still possessed considerable national resources, which, properly used, could have put it on the road to recovery. But many of these resources "were locked up by the system of government, the organization of society, and the culture" of the ancien régime. "It took the Revolution to release them."[7]

Immense Social Inequalities

Another potential resource that remained unused was the power of the French people. They were mostly poor or lower middle class and had long suffered blatant exploitation and unequal treatment under the old social-political system. Indeed, the social structure of the ancien régime was highly class-oriented, inflexible, and often unjust. Over time more and more average French had become unhappy with the existing order. As it was in other parts of Europe, May explains, in France that order

was anchored firmly on the assumption of human inequality. By reason of birth or calling, it was believed, [people] belonged to precise social castes in keeping with the will and the wish of the Almighty. Broadly speaking, there were two social categories: the privileged and the rest of humanity. The privileged element, in turn, was divided into the churchmen, or First Estate, and the aristocracy, the Second Estate. . . . More than [twenty-six million] Frenchmen, bourgeoisie [middle class], artisans, town laborers, and country folk, were grouped in the unprivileged Third Estate.[8]

The numbers of people in the other estates were much smaller—only about 100,000 clergy and perhaps 400,000 nobles. Thus, the Third Estate comprised close to 98 percent of the country's total population.

The smallest of the three estates, the clergy, possessed a decidedly disproportionate amount of power, privilege, and influence. At least this was true of the bishops and other high-ranking churchmen, who numbered perhaps fewer than a thousand. These men were recruited directly from the aristocracy. Used to wealth and privilege, they continued to collect fat incomes, dwelt in mansions or palaces, and were exempt from paying taxes. Also, this mere handful of men owned fully one-tenth of the land in France, some 20,000 square miles (51,800 sq. km). The average bishop spent most of his time enjoying the good life and knew little about his diocese and the needs and problems of its members.

Meanwhile, the lowly monks and parish priests, who made little money, did most of the actual church work. In return, they were far more liked and respected than their bosses. (Not surprisingly, therefore, most of the lower clergymen sided with the common people during the Revolution.)

The King, Queen, and Nobles

The Second Estate, made up of the royal family and the nobles, was in many ways even more privileged than the high clergy. The king had a number of absolute powers supposedly granted by God. At his own personal whim, the king could declare and wage war, dispense justice (including throwing anyone he pleased into prison), conduct foreign policy, make new laws, and tax his subjects. He also owned vast tracts of land to use for his own needs and pleasures.

The degree to which these absolute powers and extensive privileges could be misused was exemplified by Louis XV, who ruled France from 1715 to 1774. Well-meaning, but incompetent and arrogant, he reasserted his ancestral authority in a 1766 speech. "It is to me alone that legislative power belongs," he said in part. "The whole public order emanates from me, and the rights and interests of the nation . . . are necessarily joined with mine and rest only in my hands."[9]

Louis led the nation into numerous wars (including the Seven Years War), which plunged France into debt. He became widely disliked by most of his subjects.

The public image of the monarchy deteriorated even further under Louis's successor, Louis XVI (reigned 1774-1792). At first, the younger Louis and his queen, Marie-Antoinette, were popular. The French people initially saw him as caring and pious and her, as beautiful

King Louis XVI and Queen Marie-Antoinette quickly lost their popularity as their subjects came to see their weak and wasteful ways.

and compassionate, but these impressions proved to be both superficial and fleeting. The new king turned out to be slow-witted and indecisive, while Marie-Antoinette was a frivolous spendthrift who regularly shirked her royal duties. These royals eventually came to be widely seen as weak, wasteful, and symbols of a corrupt, outmoded monarchy.

Self-indulgence and waste also became the hallmarks of the French aristocracy. The leading nobles, members of ancient upper-class families, lived on immense estates that generated huge yearly incomes. They alone were allowed to serve in the Church's highest offices and to command military units. They were also exempt from paying the *taille*, a direct tax that heavily burdened

the peasants, and they possessed numerous ancient privileges, including control of local courts, rentals of land and houses, hunting rights, corn mills, wine presses, and bread ovens. These extensive privileges that wealthy lords enjoyed were among the many feudal obligations the peasants traditionally owed these nobles. In addition, most lords kept detailed records of peasant families and the obligations they owed. These records gave the nobles legal leverage and the upper hand when disputes occurred.

Only one major wedge divided the king from the hereditary nobles. To keep these traditional aristocrats from gaining too much state power, previous French kings had elevated the rank of a few middle-class families, creating a small but powerful "new aristocracy." Almost all of the king's chief ministers came from this group, whose members the older landed nobles (those who owned large amounts of land) resented.

The Third Estate

The many feudal and other privileges enjoyed by France's king and nobles were frequently exacted at the expense of commoners, the members of the Third Estate, which was divided into two rather distinct groups. The first, numbering about 400,000 or so, was the middle class (bourgeoisie), including merchants, money-lenders, ship own-

ers, shopkeepers, craftsmen, lawyers, doctors, and writers. Some made only moderate livings, while others were well-to-do. But all shared the burdens of high taxes and low social status, both of which they hated with a passion. Members of the middle class wanted to live in a society in which money and merit, not the accident of birth, determined social rank and privilege. (This wish would be partly fulfilled, for men from the bourgeoisie would end up largely running the Revolution.)

The rest of the Third Estate was comprised of the peasants, who made up the vast bulk of the population. These folks did most of the menial labor, paid

Peasants, like the ones pictured here, made up the majority of the Third Estate in France.

most of the taxes, and lived basic, poor, and uncertain lives. A majority of them, says May, "operated only small farms, sufficient merely to supply the necessities of their personal families, if indeed that. [Other peasants] hired themselves out as day laborers. Underemployment was a chronic evil in rural France. When crop yields were short, many poor peasants were reduced to beggary or actually starved."[10]

These difficulties and inequalities within France's traditional social order had been a source of discontent for a long time. But most people had simply

Jean-Jacques Rousseau was just one of several Enlightenment thinkers whose ideas found acceptance in France.

accepted them as inevitable and unchangeable. As the country's financial problems worsened at all levels in the 1760s, 1770s, and 1780s, however, tensions within all social classes grew more pronounced. "The French social pyramid was riddled with contradictions both within and between its constituent parts," scholar George Rudé explains. It had

an aristocracy that, though privileged and mostly wealthy, was deeply resentful of its long exclusion from [high state] office; a bourgeoisie that, though enjoying increasing prosperity, was denied the social status . . . commensurate with its wealth; and peasants who (in part at least) were becoming more literate and independent, yet were still regarded as a general beast of burden, despised and over-taxed. Moreover, these conflicts and the tensions they engendered were becoming sharper as the century went on.[11]

The Onrush of Modern Ideas

Also contributing to the growth of discontent in eighteenth-century France was the spread of new social and philosophical ideas that challenged the legitimacy of the old order. These ideas sprang from what came to be known as the European Enlightenment. It was a movement of thinkers and writers, most of them English and French, who strongly influ-

The Doctrine of
Separation of Powers

Frenchman Charles de Montesquieu was among the more influential thinkers of the European Enlightenment. In his 1748 treatise The Spirit of the Laws *he argued that a just government should be divided into three independent parts, the legislative, executive, and judicial:*

When legislative power is united with executive power in a single person or in a single body of the magistracy, there is no liberty, because one can fear that the same monarch or senate that makes tyrannical laws will execute them tyrannically. Nor is there liberty if the power of judging is not separate from legislative power and from executive power. If it were joined to legislative power, the power over the life and liberty of the citizens would be arbitrary, for the judge would be the legislator. If it were joined to executive power, the judge could have the force of an oppressor. All would be lost if the same man or the same body of principal men . . . exercised these three powers, that of making laws, that of executing public resolutions, and that of judging the crimes or the disputes of individuals.

Quoted in Diane Ravitch and Abigail Thernstrom, eds., *The Democracy Reader: Classic and Modern Speeches, Essays, Poems, Declarations, and Documents on Freedom and Human Rights Worldwide*. New York: Harper-Collins, 1992, p. 41.

enced people and institutions throughout Europe and the Americas. These thinkers (referred to as *philosophes* in France) called for the universal adoption of certain rights they argued are basic. Among them are religious freedom; fair, just, representative government; and freedom of speech and expression. They also stressed the importance of reason, science, and regular social and political reform in the creation of a more enlightened society and world.

Chief among the French Enlightenment thinkers were Francois-Marie Arouet, better known simply as Voltaire (1694–1778), Charles de Montesquieu (1689–1755), and Jean-Jacques Rousseau (1712–1778). (Rousseau was born in Switzerland but lived and worked in France.) These men argued, variously, that the Church was corrupt and should be reformed; all human beings are by nature equal and good (though subject to corruption) and have the right to control their own destiny; and the principal role of a nation's government is to meet the needs of its citizenry.

Such ideas, then widely viewed as radical, found fertile soil for growth in France. There, writes scholar John H. Stewart, the middle class was extremely "desirous of change." Moreover, many of its members were literate and eagerly read and discussed the writings of the philosophes. These writings reached the people through a number of media outlets, Stewart points out. "Coffee shops [cafés] provided meeting places where people might discuss current trends, where news could be disseminated, [and] where even the illiterate could learn what was taking place. Masonic lodges [private clubs] likewise afforded an excellent [atmosphere] for the exchange of ideas and opinions." Other important outlets for exchanging news and ideas included France's many salons (gatherings of literary and artistic people) and the distribution of short, but often controversial, pamphlets. The latter, says Stewart, "could be written and printed rapidly, circulated inexpensively, and passed easily from reader to reader."[12]

Thus, in short, in the late 1780s the French people were, on the whole, unhappy with the status quo, and some of them had strong ideas about alternative systems. The question was not whether change would come, but rather how and when it would happen. As it turned out, it happened sooner than anyone expected. The king needed money badly. And he decided to ask his people for help, not realizing that this seemingly harmless act would lead both to his untimely death and the utter transformation of the society he had known.

Chapter Two

Emergence of the National Assembly

One financial adviser after another told King Louis that there was only one viable, realistic way to restore the health of France's ailing economy. He would have to place a tax on the vast lands owned by the nobility and church. Both of these groups had long been exempt from land taxes, and they continued to refuse to pay them. They politely, but forcefully, pointed out that the only legal way the king could force them to pay such taxes was to call a meeting of the Estates General.

The Estates General was the French version of medieval Europe's great councils. In these large-scale meetings held from time to time, chosen delegates from various social classes presented their grievances to their rulers; and the rulers promised to provide remedies or reforms. (In England, these meetings became increasingly regular and evolved into the representative legislature known as Parliament). In medieval France, which grew into a powerful monarchy in the 1400s and 1500s, the Estates General had decreased in influence after its last meeting had occurred in 1614, 160 years before Louis became king.

The wealthy notables who had scoffed at paying Louis the taxes he wanted were sure that he would not go so far as to resurrect that seemingly defunct institution. In their view, the king had more to lose than to gain by doing so. After all, such a gathering would allow the members of the Third Estate to present their various grievances to the government. And the king had enough problems to deal with already without creating more.

However, Louis was in such dire need of money that he proceeded to call the bluff of the nobles and bishops. Late in 1788 he called for a new meeting of the Estates General to be held the following

A scene from the Estates General meeting called by Louis in 1788. This meeting set the stage for the beginning of the French Revolution.

spring. His official summons for the council said in part:

> Beloved and loyal supporters, we require the assistance of our faithful subjects to overcome the difficulties in which we find ourselves concerning the current state of our finances, and to establish, as we so wish, a constant and invariable order in all branches of government that concern the happiness of our subjects and the prosperity of the realm. These great motives have induced us to summon the Assembly of the Estates of all Provinces [i.e., the Estates General] to inform us of the wishes and grievances of our people.[13]

With these words Louis unwittingly set in motion a social-political chain reaction he would be powerless to stop.

Powerful Forces Unleashed

Just as the nobles and churchmen had underestimated Louis, he now made the same mistake in regard to the Third Estate. Evidently he thought that its representatives would obediently come to Paris and present some minimal grievances; he would make a show of promising to address them; and finally, they would approve his plan to levy new taxes on the wealthy and then go home.

What the king did not foresee was that the Third Estate might not want to dutifully bow to him and leave. It did not occur to him that its members might assert themselves against the established order. Perhaps partly because the monarchy had, by habit, insulated itself from life and thought among the commoners, the king did not realize that powerful forces had been unleashed in the form of the people's raised hopes. Many French saw the upcoming meeting as a sign that the government was ready to hear and remedy their grievances. Some even dared to hope that they would take part in instituting a new, fairer social-political system. To them, the royal summons to the Estates General "was a recognition of the fact that reform was imperative," as historian R.K. Gooch puts it. "It was also a recognition of the fact that the king could not, without the collaboration of the nation, effect real reform. . . . The king's acceptance, however reluctant, of the direction and force of public opinion aroused high hopes in the country."[14]

These expectations that the upcoming meeting might bring positive reforms were expressed in numerous gatherings of small groups of citizens in the cities and towns. People's hopes and optimism about the meeting also manifested themselves in the circulation of hundreds, perhaps even thousands, of pamphlets. Arthur Young, an English landowner who was staying in France at this time observed:

The business going forward in the pamphlet shops is incredible. . . . Every hour produces something new. Thirteen [pamphlets] came

out today, sixteen yesterday, and ninety-two last week. . . . The spirit of reading political tracts, they say, spreads into the provinces, so that all the presses of France are equally employed. . . . It is easy to conceive the spirit that must be raised among the people. But the coffee houses . . . present yet more singular and astonishing spectacles. They are not only crowded within, but other expectant crowds are at the doors and windows [lis-

An illustration of France divided into the Three Estates—the nobility, the clergy, and the peasantry.

tening] to various orators. . . . The eagerness with which they are heard and the thunder of applause they receive for every sentiment . . . against the present government cannot easily be imagined.[15]

Bold and Provocative Ideas

The representatives of the three estates gathered in Paris in late April 1789 in anticipation of the great meeting, which was slated to convene at Versailles, just outside the city. The opening ceremonies, in which the king was to formally greet the delegates, took place on May 2. It was on this day that Louis made his first serious mistake. Forgetting, or perhaps not caring, that he was dealing from a position of weakness and badly needed the commoners' support, he treated them shabbily. First, he warmly, and with appropriate pomp, greeted the delegates of the nobility and clergy. But then, he rudely kept the delegates of the Third Estate waiting for three hours. When he finally met with them, he maintained a cold, aloof posture as they filed by him one by one. According to noted scholar of the Revolution, Christopher Hibbert, "The king, standing between his two brothers, could not bring himself to address a single word to any of them other than one old man of exceptionally benign appearance, to whom he said, "Good morning, good man." The others, having made their bows, turned away, feeling much disheartened by the king's inability to display the least indication of friendliness."[16]

It is possible that Louis's incivility was due in part to the fact that he was not looking forward to hearing the commoners' complaints. He was aware, after all, that they had come bearing *cahiers de doléances*, lists of grievances that they expected him to consider in exchange for supporting his tax initiative. These grievances, compiled in various towns across the realm, included numerous and diverse requests and demands. Typical were appeals for regular meetings of the Estates General, lower taxes, and freedom of the press. Concerning the last of these, a group of commoners from Paris declared that "liberty of the press must be granted, on condition that authors sign their manuscripts, that the printer's name shall appear, and that both shall be responsible for the consequences of publication."[17] Another grievance, from the town of Vire (located several miles west of Paris), asked for a more even-handed justice system. "Justice [should] be free of charge [and] civil and criminal edicts [should] be reformed [and] crime alone, and not the social standing of the criminal, [should] determine the sentence, and . . . no citizen may, under the pretext of any [social or aristocratic] privilege . . . be brought before any other than his natural judge."[18]

Such requests, though somewhat daring for the time, were actually among the tamer ideas and statements circulating among the crowds of commoners. Emmanuel-Joseph Sieyès (commonly called Abbé Sieyès), a delegate of and spokesman for the Third Estate,

A Radical Attacks the Nobility

One of the most controversial pamphlets circulating in France in the weeks just prior to the Revolution's outbreak was "What is the Third Estate?" by the outspoken Abbé Sieyès. In this section, he attacks the aristocratic class and its traditional privileges.

It is not possible in the number of all the elementary parts of a nation to find a place for the caste of nobles. . . . The worst possible arrangement of all would be where not alone isolated individuals, but a whole class of citizens should take pride in remaining motionless in the midst of the general movement, and should consume the best part of the product without bearing any part in its production. Such a class is surely estranged to the nation by its indolence [laziness]. . . . Is it not evident that the noble order has privileges and expenditures which it dares to call its rights, but which are apart from the rights of the great body of citizens? It departs there from the common order, from the common law. So its civil rights make of it an isolated people in the midst of the great nation.

Quoted in "Sieyès: 'What Is the Third Estate?' (1789)," Liberty, Equality, Fraternity: Exploring the French Revolution (http://chnm.gmu.edu/revolution/d/280/).

Abbé Sieyès's pamphlet titled "What is the Third Estate?" inspired many of the Third Estate delegates to demand change from the nobility.

The Unprecedented Democratic Spectacle

The cahiers, *or lists of grievances, drawn up by local groups of citizens and presented to the government at the Estates General, were highly progressive and controversial for their time, as explained by one of the leading scholars of the Revolution, William Doyle:*

The *cahiers* produced a picture of the outlook and preoccupations of a whole nation unique in Europe before the twentieth century. And the very fact of being asked to articulate their grievances and aspirations (with the implicit promise of redress) concentrated the minds of everybody involved on the seriousness of what was at stake. . . . The drafting of the *cahiers* drew in people throughout the country. The [local] elections of [representatives to the Estates General in] 1789 were the most democratic spectacle ever seen in the history of Europe, and nothing comparable occurred again until far into the next century.

William Doyle, *The Oxford History of the French Revolution.* Oxford, England: Clarendon, 2002, p. 97.

had recently published a pamphlet titled "What is the Third Estate?" Many of the delegates had read it, and they agreed with its major points, including these bold and provocative ones:

Who then shall dare to say that the Third Estate has not within itself all that is necessary for the formation of a complete nation? It is the strong and robust man who has one arm still shackled. If the privileged order should be abolished, the nation would be nothing less, but something more. Therefore, what is the Third Estate? Everything; but an everything shackled and oppressed. What would it be without the privileged order? Everything, but an everything free and flourishing. Nothing can succeed without it, [and] everything would be infinitely better without the others. It is not sufficient to show that privileged persons, far from being useful to the nation, cannot but enfeeble and injure it. It is necessary to prove further that the noble order does not enter at all into the social organization; that it may indeed be a burden upon the nation, but that it cannot of itself constitute a nation.[19]

Demands for New Rules

Before the people's grievances could be formally presented, however, the delegates of the three estates had to agree on acceptable rules for debate and voting. And even before this step could be taken, tradition dictated that the delegates' credentials had to be examined and verified. This formality was designed to make sure that every person at the meeting had been properly chosen by his peers for this important task. Back in 1614 each estate had briefly met separately and checked the credentials of its own members. And now, in 1789, the nobles and churchmen proceeded to do the same.

But the delegates of the Third Estate were uncomfortable with the procedure. First, how could they be sure that what went on in the other two meetings was fair? Also, they argued, if the Estates General truly represented the entire realm, should not everyone's credentials be open to examination by all three estates? Following this reasoning, the commoners refused to present their credentials until the other two estates agreed to an open process.

There was also a lot of talk among the commoners about voting procedure for the convention. In the past, each estate had had a single, collective voice amounting to one vote. Not surprisingly, aiming to maintain their monopoly on power, the nobles and clergy had always voted together, two-to-one, against the Third Estate. The commoners now strongly objected to this approach. They demanded that the rules be changed to give each and every delegate of the convention a vote. And because the nobles had 285 delegates, the clergy 308, and the commoners 621, that would give the Third Estate a majority voice.

When it looked as if the nobles and clergy were not going to bend on the credentials and voting issues, the members of the Third Estate became increasingly irritated and bold. They made overtures to members of the first two estates, asking them to join the third. A group of commoners went to the churchmen's meeting and said, "the gentlemen of the Commons invite the gentlemen of the clergy, in the name of the God of Peace and for the national interest, to meet them in their hall to consult upon the means of bringing about the concord [peaceful agreement] which is so vital at this moment for the public welfare."[20]

At first these invitations went unanswered. But on June 10 the earnest and by now quite impatient Sieyès proposed that the commoners strike out on their own. If the other two estates would not join the third, he said, they should forfeit their rights to speak for the nation. This audacious move had the desired effect. Three days later, on June 13, three priest-delegates of the First Estate appeared at the door of the hall where the commoners were meeting. They were welcomed by tumultuous applause. In the next two days sixteen more clergymen joined the Third Estate.

In the Name of the French People

Emboldened, the delegates of the Third Estate now reasoned, with some justification, that their ranks no longer represented only the commoners. Rather, in their view, they stood for the wishes and rights of the vast majority of French of all classes. So on June 17, in the name of the French people, they took the extraordinary step of issuing a short document in which they declared their body to be the National Assembly of France. "In a few deliberate and coldly logical phrases," scholar Leo Gershoy points out, "they set aside the entire theory and practice of a government and society based upon privileged orders and asserted the democratic theory of [superior] numbers and of popular sovereignty."[21] Among these bold phrases were the following:

Delegates of the Third Estate meet on June 17, 1789, during the first National Assembly of France.

Choosing a Name for the New Legislature

After deciding to take matters into their own hands and form a national legislative body, the revolutionaries first took up the issue of what to call that body. Some of the delegates proposed they should call themselves *The Nation*. Another suggestion was *Representatives of the French People* and another, the mouthful: *The Lawful Assembly of the Representatives of the Greater Part of the Nation Acting in the Absence of the Minor Part*. Similar suggestions included *The Representatives of the Much Greater Part of the French in the National Assembly*, and *The Representatives of Almost the Whole of the French People*. Finally, the delegates voted to adopt the far simpler *National Assembly*.

This Assembly is already composed of representatives sent directly by at least ninety-six one-hundredths [96 percent] of the nation. . . . Thus, the Assembly declares that the common work of national restoration can and must be initiated without delay by the deputies present, and that they must continue without interruption and without obstacle.[22]

In the wake of this clearly revolutionary act, shock waves rippled across the capital and in the days that followed throughout the nation and beyond. Perhaps sensing the popular will, a majority of the priests, along with a handful of aristocrats from the Second Estate, joined the new Assembly on June 19. Meanwhile, the king and his ministers, not to mention the leading nobles, were aghast and even fearful. Some urged the king to send in troops to disband the Assembly and arrest its leaders.

But Louis correctly reasoned that such a show of force might turn these upstarts into martyrs and thereby help their cause. So he took the less confrontational approach of depriving them of their meeting place. On June 20 when the Assembly's members arrived at their hall, they found the doors locked and guarded by soldiers.

Undaunted, however, the delegates hurried to a nearby indoor tennis court. There, they swore never to disband until their self-appointed task of reforming the nation was finished. That declaration, which appropriately became known as the "Tennis Court Oath," reads in part:

The National Assembly, considering that it has been called to establish the constitution of the realm, to bring about the regeneration of public order, and to maintain the true principles of the monarchy, nothing may prevent it from continuing its deliberations in any place it is forced to establish itself and, finally, the National Assembly exists wherever its members are gathered [and] decrees that all members of this assembly immediately take solemn oath never to separate, and to reassemble whenever circumstances require, until the constitution of the realm is drawn up and fixed upon solid foundations; and that said oath having been sworn, all members in general, and each one individually confirm this unwavering resolution with his signature.[23]

On the one hand, from the viewpoint of these brave men at that historic moment, the die had been cast. Unable to predict what might happen next, they were ready to suffer any consequences for what they saw as the good of their country. On the other, from the viewpoint of posterity, the French Revolution had begun.

Chapter Three

The Revolution Turns Violent

The unexpected events of May and June 1789 had created an atmosphere of anxiety and uncertainty in Paris. The commoners, along with a few members of the other two estates, had defied the king, declared themselves the National Assembly, and sworn not to disband until they had reformed the government. At this point the revolutionaries had no intention of transforming France into a democracy. Also, they did not plan, nor did they even contemplate, abolishing the monarchy. Rather, their main goal was to draft a written constitution that would guarantee all French citizens, regardless of social class, basic civil rights. Then, they ardently hoped, the king would approve the document. France would thereafter be a constitutional monarchy, in which the king's authority rested on the will of the people and their legislative representatives. In short, the protestors were optimistic that the government could and would be reformed in a peaceful manner.

The sad fact is that this nonviolent scenario might well have transpired had it not been for Louis's arrogance, imprudence, and lack of vision. Although he was willing to make some minor concessions to the protestors, he haughtily reminded all involved that he was still the king. So he had the final word. And there was only so far that he was willing to bend. In the days that followed, as both sides refused to retreat from their stated positions, tension steadily rose. Finally, violence broke out, transforming what had been a peaceful rebellion into a bloody one.

The King Offers Concessions

Louis's inability to grasp the true scope and gravity of the situation, as well as his inflexibility and lack of wisdom as a ruler, are well illustrated by his actions

The French Revolution may never have become as violent and deadly as it was if Louis XVI had been more willing to compromise with the Third Estate's demands.

in the days following the Tennis Court Oath. He failed to recognize that the men who had sworn not to disband were not merely a small, isolated group of discontented people. Rather, they in-creasingly had the silent support of and spoke for thousands, even millions, of resentful French. Apparently unable to see this big picture, Louis assumed he could ease the crisis by acceding to a few of the protestors' demands while firmly reasserting what he viewed as his legitimate, God-given authority over them.

To this end the king scheduled a meeting between himself and the delegates of the three estates on June 23, three days after the Tennis Court Oath. Louis's entrance into the hall that day was accompanied by a lavish fanfare of trumpets and rolling drums. The gathered nobles and some of the clergy cheered him; but the commoners stood silent. Then he launched into a long prepared speech, which began with a reminder of his good intentions:

I believed I had done everything in my power for the good of my people when I resolved to assemble you . . . when, one might well say, I exceeded the nation's wishes by demonstrating in advance what I wanted to do for its happiness. . . . I owe it to the common good of my realm, [and] I owe it to myself to bring an end to these

A painting commemorating the meeting of the Third Estate in which the delegates swore an oath not to separate until a constitution had been established in France.

The King Promises Reforms

When he met with the delegates of the Estates General on June 23, 1789, King Louis promised a number of reforms which, because the Revolution overshadowed him, he was never able to implement. Among others, these reforms included:

No new tax shall be created and no current tax will be extended beyond the term set by law and without consent of the nation's representatives. . . . Once the formal arrangements announced by clergy and nobility to renounce their financial privileges have been fixed . . . the king intends to sanction them so that there will be no more privileges or distinctions in the payment of financial contributions. . . . All property, without exception, will be respected. . . . His majesty will examine (with scrupulous attention) all projects presented to him concerning the administration of justice and the means to perfect civil and criminal laws.

Quoted in Georges Lefebvre and Anne Terroine, eds., *Recueil de Documents Relatifs aux Séances des États-Généraux, Vol. 1.* trans. Laura Mason. Paris: National Center of Scientific Research, 1962, pp. 278–79.

deadly divisions. It is with these resolutions, sirs, that I gather you around me. It is as common father to all my subjects, as defender of the laws of the realm, that I come to remind you of the true spirit of the laws and to repress any attacks directed against them.[24]

As the gathered delegates listened, Louis offered to negotiate a series of reforms. The Estates General would be allowed to meet on a regular basis and would have a number of financial powers. For instance, no new taxes would hereafter be imposed "without the consent of the nation's representatives." Further, the Estates General would prepare a sort of annual national budget of revenues and expenses, although it would be subject to the king's approval. The nobles and clergy would renounce their ancient financial privileges, and all French citizens would be taxed in the same manner. Louis also went on to say that "the Estates General will examine and make known to his majesty the most suitable means to reconcile liberty of the press with the respect due to religion, morals, and the honor of citizens."[25]

These and the king's other concessions and remarks completely ignored the existence of the new National Assembly. What Louis was proposing was that, except for the reforms he had just outlined, things should return to the way they had stood in May, before the Third Estate had asserted itself. And to emphasize that he was still in charge, he now reaffirmed his own authority. The three estates were to continue, per custom, to meet separately to discuss most matters. Moreover, the delegates had no right to draw up a constitution on their own, as it would be an invalid, illegal document. "None of your projects, none of your arrangements," he said, "can have the force of law without my special approbation [approval]. I am the natural guarantor of your respective rights."[26]

After finishing his speech, the king ordered everyone to leave and attend their separate meetings. Then he departed, followed by most members of the first two estates. However, the revolutionaries remained in the hall in defiance of the order. One of their leaders, Honoré Gabriel Mirabeau, told Louis's deputy, "Go tell your master that we are here by the will of the people and that we shall not stir from our seats unless forced to do so by bayonets."[27]

Prelude to Violence

On hearing about the delegates' disobedience, Louis showed restraint and did nothing. (An alternate account claims that he ordered soldiers to clear out the hall. If this was the case, they arrived after the delegates had left.) Clearly, he was unsure about how to deal with the continued defiance of his subjects, something he had never encountered before. His frustration and feelings of impotence further increased a few days later when several more clergymen and another forty-seven nobles joined the revolutionaries. In addition, rumors began to circulate in the capital that if he did not agree to allow all the estates to meet together, thousands of protestors might surround his palace. So on June 27 he gave in and announced that he would allow such joint meetings.

At this point the rebels had dramatically changed France's social-political order in only a few weeks; they had done so without resorting to violence; also, the king had offered only marginal interference. Had nothing else occurred to change this unfolding scenario, everyone's needs and demands might have been met over time. Large-scale bloodshed might have been avoided.

However, Louis proceeded to make a more forceful stand, which, under the circumstances, was bound to lead to a dangerous situation. Perhaps he feared losing his great power and wealth. Certainly some members of the royal family and a few disgruntled noblemen felt this way. They strongly urged the king to use the army to enforce his will, and he did so. In late June he ordered four regiments of soldiers to advance on Paris and Versailles. Soon afterward he called up several additional regiments, activating a force of some twenty thousand soldiers in all.

News of the approaching troops swiftly spread through the capital, significantly raising levels of tension and fear. The leaders of the Revolution were genuinely worried that the soldiers might disband the Assembly or maybe

French citizens arm themselves with guns and ammunition in fear of being attacked by the king's troops.

even ransack the city. In a speech to the Assembly on July 8, Mirabeau railed: "A large number of troops already surround us! More are arriving each day. Artillery are being brought up. . . . These preparations for war are obvious to anyone and fill every heart with indignation."[28]

As worries about an imminent attack on the city increased, many Parisians felt they must mount some sort of de-fense. This meant that they must arm themselves, if possible, with muskets and cannons. So in the next few days the city streets, already filled with pro-testers, speech-makers, and many con-fused, frightened people, became even more chaotic as groups of citizens searched for guns and ammunition. Pierre-Victor Besenval was commander of Paris's permanent garrison of royal troops at the time. At first he considered using his men to break up the protests and clear the streets. But when he realized the magnitude of the crowds and unrest, he thought better of it and ordered the soldiers not to interfere unless fired on. These troops, he later recalled,

> were the target of insulting cries, stone-throwing and pistol-shots. Several men were severely wounded, but not a single menacing gesture was made by the soldiers, so great was their respect for the order that not a drop of their fellow-citizens'

blood was to be shed. The disorder increased hourly and with it my misgivings. What decision was I to take? If I engaged my troops in Paris, I should start a civil war. Blood, precious from whatever veins it flowed, would be shed without achieving any result likely to restore calm.[29]

Capture of the Bastille

By July 14, some of the weapons-searchers had become desperate. Around

A mob of citizens looking for weapons attacks the Bastille in Paris on July 14, 1789.

ten in the morning some nine hundred of them converged on the Bastille in Paris's eastern sector. This imposing fortress-prison had once housed political prisoners arrested by the monarchy and had come to be viewed as a hated symbol of the regime's past abuses. But the structure's symbolic meaning was a secondary motive for targeting it. The gathered merchants, artisans, laborers, and soldiers (those French troops who had already defected to the revolutionary cause) were primarily interested in seizing the Bastille's considerable stores of guns and gunpowder.

At first two representatives of the mob met with the fortress's governor (commander), Bernard-René de Launay. They demanded that he allow the people to enter and collect the arms. If he agreed, there would be no need for bloodshed. But Launay hesitated to give in to the demand, partly because he felt that to do so required obtaining permission from his superiors in Versailles.

While these negotiations were going on, the crowd became increasingly restless. Tempers flared and the violence that all hoped to avoid erupted. The exact series of events that followed remains dis-

A Citizen Remembers the Bastille's Fall

In the crowd of Parisians who marched on the Bastille on July 14, 1789, was a man named Keversau, who later recalled the following events:

Veteran armies . . . have never performed greater prodigies [examples] of valor than this leaderless multitude . . . workmen of all trades who, mostly ill-equipped and unused to arms, boldly affronted the fire from the ramparts and seemed to mock the thunderbolts the enemy hurled at them. . . . The attackers, having demolished the first drawbridge and brought their guns into position against the second, could not fail to capture the fort. . . . The people, infuriated by the treachery of the Governor, who had fired on their representatives . . . continued to advance, firing as they went up to the drawbridge leading to the interior of the fort. A Swiss officer addressing the attackers through a sort of loop-hole near the drawbridge asked permission to leave the fort with the honors of war. "No, no!" they cried. . . . About two minutes later one of the [guards] opened the gate behind the drawbridge and asked what we wanted. "The surrender of the Bastille," was the answer, on which he let us in.

Quoted in Georges Pernoud and Sabine Flaissier, eds., *The French Revolution*. trans. Richard Graves. New York: Capricorn, 1961, pp. 31–35.

puted because surviving eyewitness reports are somewhat contradictory, as each side claimed the other fired first. The following account, by one of the officers stationed in the Bastille, though lacking in specific detail, is probably fairly accurate. He confirms what all the accounts agree on, that Launay eventually surrendered rather than risk the massacre of himself and his men.

> [Members of the mob] cut the chains holding the drawbridge, and it fell open. . . . After having easily dropped the bridge, they easily knocked down the door with axes and entered into the courtyard. [There was a prolonged exchange of gunfire that killed a number of people.] I stationed my men to the left of the gate. . . . I waited for the moment when the governor [was] to [act] and I was very surprised to see him send four veterans to the gates to open them and to lower the bridges. The crowd entered right away and disarmed us in an instant. In the castle, archives were thrown from the windows and everything was pillaged.[30]

The brief, but momentous, battle resulted in ninety-eight dead in the crowd, along with several wounded, and six dead among the defenders. Afterward, angry Parisians, convinced that Launay had fired first, dragged him through the streets and then stabbed and shot him to death. Though small-scale as battles go, the Bastille's

fall had an enormous impact on the unfolding crisis, and thereby on posterity. (Ever since, the French have celebrated July 14 as their independence day.) Put simply, Paris had fallen completely into the hands of the revolutionaries. King Louis had enough troops to storm and retake the city, to be sure, but at what cost would this be accomplished? This was a question that echoed far and wide, including through the ranks of those troops. The king's officers soberly advised him that if he gave the order for the soldiers to fire on their fellow citizens, it would likely be disobeyed. William Doyle explains the meaning of this crucial turning point:

> Louis XVI's acceptance of that advice marked the end of royal authority. The monarch recognized that he no longer had the power to enforce his will. He was therefore compelled finally to accept all that had been done since mid-June. The Estates General had gone. They had been replaced by a single National Assembly . . . claiming sovereignty in the name of the nation and a mission to endow France with a constitution.[31]

Accordingly, with a mixture of reluctance and resignation, the king ordered his troops to withdraw.

The Great Fear

Though significant, this triumph of the people over the monarchy did not mark the end of the Revolution. Instead, it proved to be merely the end of the

Ancient Feudal Rights Abolished

On August 4, 1789, the National Assembly abolished the feudal rights and privileges the nobles had long enjoyed. The decree reads in part:

Feudal rights and dues deriving from real or personal *mainmorte* [a peasant's property that at his death passed to his noble lord] and personal servitude, and those representative thereof, are abolished. . . . The exclusive right of hunting and open warrens is likewise abolished; and every proprietor [landowner] has the right to destroy . . . on his property only, every kind of game. . . . All [feudal] courts of justice are suppressed. . . . Tithes [taxes to support the Church] of every kind and dues which take the place thereof are abolished. . . . All citizens may be admitted, without distinction of birth, to all [religious], civil, and military employments and offices.

Quoted in John H. Stewart, ed., *A Documentary Survey of the French Revolution*. New York: Macmillan, 1971, p. 107.

The National Assembly meeting on August 4, 1789, abolishes the feudal rights and privileges of the nobles.

beginning of a long, tumultuous, and at times violent national transformation. Indeed, the next round of turmoil began almost immediately. When news of the events in Paris filtered into the countryside, large portions of the nation were drawn into the unfolding drama. Rumors spread from one village and town to another. One quite incorrectly claimed that the king had ordered his troops into rural areas to suppress dissent among the peasants.

As a result, mass hysteria took hold in many areas. It became known as the *Grande Peur*, or "Great Fear." Tens of thousands of peasants armed themselves with whatever weapons they could find and barricaded themselves against the impending invasion. When it did not come, they went on a rampage. Their main targets were the chief symbols of the old feudal authority—the mansions of the rich lords who had long held so much power over the lives of millions. The marauders attacked and in some cases burned these wealthy manors.

But "above all," as one expert points out, they sought out the rooms where "records of feudal obligations were held." Destroying these records, the peasants reasoned, would deal a blow to the aristocrats' power to exploit the populace. "The rooms were ransacked, their contents burned, and distantly glimpsed smoke palls from bonfires of legal papers made their own contributions to the general panic."[32]

The nobles sitting in the Assembly in Paris were appalled by the mayhem in the countryside and became determined to stop it. In a dramatic gesture on the evening of August 4, all of the aristocrats in the Assembly renounced their feudal rights. In addition, that body promptly voted to abolish all ancient feudal rights in France. Then, carried away by a spirit of justice and fairness for all, the legislators went on to remove other existing barriers among the social classes. "All citizens may be admitted, without distinction of birth, to all [religious], civil, and military employments and offices,"[33] one provision stated. This meant that all French citizens were now equal under the law.

In retrospect it is clear that the work of the Assembly that night averted much loss of life and property. When news of the new, enlightened laws reached the countryside, the rioting subsided. The members of the Assembly now turned their attention to what seemed to them the most important act—creating the new constitution for the country.

Chapter Four

A Constitution Forged in Blood

In August 1789 the deputies (members) of France's National Assembly began the project that they viewed as most crucial—drafting a new constitution for the country. Most of them agreed on the first step in this process. Namely, the new blueprint for national government should rest upon the solid foundation of a declaration of basic civil rights. Further, these rights should be similar in nature and scope to the ones stated in the Declaration of Independence, which American patriot Thomas Jefferson had written in 1776.

The Assembly soon completed both the declaration of rights and the new Constitution. But these documents turned out to be forged in blood. Though their authors were well-meaning and their provisions enlightened, neither the deputies nor the noble ideals they had stated could prevent continued outbreaks of violence. Some of it, including massacres of innocent people, was

spontaneous; but other bloodshed, including the brutal execution of the king, was coldly planned and carried out.

The *Declaration of Rights*

At least at first, the deputies of the National Assembly had no intention of resorting to or condoning violence. In fact, most of them assumed or hoped that the Bastille's fall in July and the riots in the countryside that had followed it represented the last blood that would be shed in the Revolution. Indeed, there seemed to be no need for further unrest. After all the Assembly was hard at work on a document that would address the fundamental rights of all French. There also was an optimistic feeling among the deputies that most citizens would see it as the basis of a new era of peace and brotherhood.

For models for their rights declaration, the deputies had the American De-

The French revolutionaries used the American Declaration of Independence as one of the models when developing their Declaration of the Rights of Man and of the Citizen.

claration of Independence and the bills of rights enacted by Virginia and other U.S. states in the 1770s. (The U.S. federal Bill of Rights was not ratified until 1791.) The French legislators deeply admired these documents. However, they wanted the French version to be even more sweeping in its recognition of human freedoms. One member of the Assembly remarked that the Americans "have set a great example in the new hemisphere. Let us give one to the universe!"[34]

The first draft of the new document was completed on August 27, 1789. Titled the *Declaration of the Rights of Man and of the Citizen*, it begins with these stirring words:

> The representatives of the French people . . . considering that ignorance, forgetfulness, or contempt of the rights of man are the sole causes of public miseries and the corruption of governments, have resolved to set forth in a solemn declaration the natural, inalienable, and sacred rights of man . . . in order that the demands of the citizens . . . may always take the direction of maintaining the constitution and welfare of all.[35]

The document goes on to list basic civil rights, each based to one degree or another on the sentiments of the same Enlightenment thinkers who had inspired the American founding fathers. Like the American bills of rights, the French version established specific civil liberties, including the right to be presumed innocent until proven guilty,

equality of all citizens under the law, freedom of religion, and freedom of speech. The article guaranteeing the latter reads: "The free communication of ideas and opinions is one of the most precious of the rights of man. Every citizen can then freely speak, write, and print, subject to responsibility for the abuse of this freedom in the cases determined by law."[36]

In a surprisingly short amount of time, the French legislators created a statement of democratic principles that turned France's centuries-old system of absolute monarchy on its head. The inherited rights of a few privileged aristocrats were no longer meaningful or usable. In their place, the authors of the declaration substituted the notion that, as scholar Lynn Hunt puts it,

> the legitimacy of government must flow from the guarantee of individual rights by the law. Under the monarchy, legitimacy depended on the king's will and his maintenance of a historic order that granted privileges according to rank and status. Most remarkably, the deputies of 1789 endeavored to make a statement of universal application, rather than one particularly or uniquely French, and it is that universality that has ensured the continuing resonance of the document.[37]

Trouble at the Palace

Despite their democratic zeal, the vast majority of the Assembly's deputies still did not plan to create a democracy like that of the Untied States. Rather, the French leaders expected that the new rights they had enunciated would work within the framework of a constitutional monarchy. In that system the king would still be the ceremonial head of state. And one of his duties would be to authorize the Assembly's major statements and legislation.

For these reasons, the deputies wanted Louis to provide his official approval of the *Declaration of Rights*. Thus, they presented the document to him on October 2, 1789. To their disappointment, however, he told them that he needed time to look it over in detail and that he would render his opinion on the matter later. But how much later, the legislators wondered? Some deputies, as well as many other French, were worried that the king might be stalling for a sinister reason. Perhaps, they suspected, he was planning to mobilize the army once again in a desperate bid to reinstate his former powers.

Motivated partly by such concerns, as well as angry over recent bread shortages, one sector of the populace suddenly and impulsively took action.

French women march to Versailles on October 5, 1789, to protest the inaction of Louis XVI during bread shortages.

a Versaille a Versaille. du 5. Octobre 1789.

On October 5 a large group of Parisian women marched to Louis's palace at Versailles. First, they demanded that he use his wealth and influence to provide bread for hungry families. Also they said they were there to support the Revolution and its principles. They had heard that some of the king's officers had made insulting remarks about the Revolution, and they demanded that these officers be punished. Furthermore, the women asserted, in the future the royal family's guards should be drawn solely from Parisian soldiers loyal to the Revolution.

Worried that the assembled women might become violent and hurt his family, Louis gave in. He agreed to provide bread and thereafter to approve the Assembly's decrees and demands. The women did not trust him, however, and refused to take him at his word. They forced him and his family to move to the old palace, the Tuileries, in Paris, where they could keep a closer eye on his activities. The queen's foster brother, Joseph Weber, witnessed the march back to Paris and later described, "the horror of a cold, somber, rainy day, the infamous militia splattering through the mud, the harpies, monsters with human faces [i.e., the women protestors], the captive monarch and his family . . . dragged along by guards."[38]

The New Constitution

The king and his family remained under what amounted to house arrest at the Tuileries for many months as the Assembly's deputies worked diligently to finish writing the new Constitution. That document affirmed that France would be a constitutional monarchy in which the king would be the head of state. However, he would for the most part have to do the bidding of the national legislature, which would hold most of the real government authority.

The Assembly also abolished the ancient French provinces. In their place, it created eighty-three local areas of roughly equal size called "departments." Each department was subdivided into smaller units, including "districts" and "communes."

In addition, those drawing up the new Constitution addressed many of the democratic concepts outlined in the *Declaration of Rights*. For instance, they discussed the process of granting religious freedom to people of all faiths in the country. Particularly controversial in this regard was the situation of French Jews. The deputies had no argument with the idea of giving religious freedom to all citizens. The problem was that historically the Jews, widely hated by Christians across Europe, had never been considered true or complete French citizens. On January 28, 1790, a group of leading Jews presented the Assembly with the "Petition of Jews of Paris, Alsace, and Lorraine." It argued that Jews *were* legitimately citizens and should be accorded the same rights as Catholics and Protestants:

The time has passed when one could say that it was only the dominant religion that could grant access to advantages [and] the lucrative and honorable posts in society. For a long time . . . the Protestants had no civil standing in France. Today, they [are] reestablished in the possession of this status. They are assimilated to the Catholics in everything . . . . Why [not grant similar status to] the Jews? In general, civil rights are entirely independent from religious principles. And all men of whatever religion . . . we say, equally able to serve the fatherland, defend its interests, [and] contribute to its splendor, should all equally have the title and the rights of citizen.[39]

Regardless of this reasoned argument, the deputies did not grant the Jews religious freedom in the Constitution's initial draft. French Jews were not granted citizenship and full rights until September 1791.

Intrigue and War

The Jews were not the only French who were disappointed by the new Constitution and the political system it had created. Most of the wealthiest nobles were disgruntled over the loss of their privileges, and a number of them fled France and settled in neighboring countries. There, they began inciting a counterrevolution that they hoped would restore France to its former state.

Among these so-called *émigrés* was the Count of Artois, the king's younger brother, who eventually managed to convince Louis to try to escape the country. On the night of June 20, 1791, the king and his family disguised themselves as servants and set out toward France's northeastern border. However, the revolutionary authorities discovered what was happening. They caught up to the royals and brought them back to Paris, where an angry mob denounced Louis as a traitor.

The king's attempted flight did much more than make him more unpopular than ever with the people. The incident also proved to be a difficult political situation that divided many of the revolutionaries. Scholars Laura Mason and Tracey Rizzo explain:

By fleeing, Louis undermined his image as a monarch loyal to the Revolution. Revolutionaries would henceforth have sound reasons to mistrust him. As well, he encouraged counter-revolution, for opponents within and outside France could and did claim that the king was being held captive by a Revolution of which he wanted no part. Finally, and perhaps most dangerously, the revolutionaries themselves had been divided. . . . Henceforth there would be two visible parties of revolution—those who would cling to the constitutional monarchy . . . and those who would press with growing resistance for a republic and were willing to call on the crowd to achieve it.[40]

Thus, the cause of French constitutional monarchy was already weakened when the Assembly finished drafting

As Louis XVI and his family attempt to flee France, they are arrested and forced to return to Paris for Louis to stand trial.

the Constitution in September 1791. On October 1 that body disbanded itself to make way for the new, so-called Legislative Assembly created in that document. The new legislature was indeed more anti-monarchy than the old one. The most radical wing of the Assembly was a left-wing political club, or clique, known as the Jacobins. The term "Jacobins" derived from the fact that Dominican friars were called Jacobins. The deputies in the club held meetings in a Dominican monastery in Paris. They were intent on rooting out and crushing all counterrevolutionary forces and replacing the constitutional monarchy with a more democratic republic.

The Jacobins did not always agree with one another, however, and steadily divided into two groups. One, the Girondins, was only moderately radical and fairly open to discussion and compromise. The other, nicknamed the "Mountain," was more extreme and uncompromising. Its members, who championed the poor and discontented urban masses, were led by two earnest and crafty lawyers, Georges-Jacques Danton and Maximilien Robespierre.

Initially, the Girondins had control of the Assembly. One of their first official acts was to demand that all *émigrés* return to France at once or else forfeit their property. There was no response to this demand. So on April 20, 1792, the Assembly declared war on Austria, where many of the counterrevolutionary *émigrés* had settled. (Austria was also Marie-Antoinette's homeland.) Austria's ally, Prussia, then entered the war against France.

The onset of the war made many French more fearful and open to committing radical and violent acts in the name of patriotism. When a Prussian general threatened to destroy Paris, for example, an angry mob massacred more than twelve hundred prisoners in the city jails, mistaking them for counterrevolutionaries. An extreme left-wing journalist named Jean-Paul Marat helped to incite these slayings. One eyewitness, Nicolas-Edme Restif de la Bretonne, later wrote:

There had been a pause in the murders [and] I told myself that it was over at last. Finally, I saw a woman appear, as white as a sheet, being helped by a [prison guard]. They [the killers] said to her harshly: "Shout 'Vive la nation!' [Long live the nation!]" "No! No!" she said. They made her climb up on a pile of corpses. One of the killers grabbed the [guard]

An Argument for Going to War

In January 1792 the deputies in the Convention hotly debated whether to go to war with Austria. This is an excerpt from a pro-war speech made by J.P. Brissot.

It is necessary to make war now. We are sure of success in being the first to attack. All the advantages await us on enemy territory. All the disasters will follow us in our homes. Furthermore, gentlemen, all that can be said on this question can be reduced to this. [Either] the emperor [of Austria] wants war, or he only wants it in the spring, or he does not want it at all. If he wants it, it is necessary [for us to attack first]. If he only wants it next spring, it is still necessary to hasten to prevent him. If he does not want it at all, it is necessary to force him to [fight]. Therefore, in each case war is necessary.

Quoted in Laura Mason and Tracey Rizzo, *The French Revolution: A Document Collection*. Boston: Houghton Mifflin, 1999, p. 164.

and pushed him away. . . . They repeated that she must shout "Vive la nation." With disdain, she refused. Then one of the killers grabbed her, tore away her dress, and ripped open her stomach. She fell and was finished off by the others. Never could I have imagined such horror [and] I fainted. When I came to, I saw [her] bloody [severed] head. . . . What pointless cruelty![41]

The Vanishing Shadow of Royalty

This was not the end of what many French came to see as senseless violence. Eventually, the extreme Jacobins of the Mountain joined forces with a

With the public execution of Louis XVI on January 21, 1793, the legislators hoped that the French monarchy would also come to an end.

A Plea for the King's Life

Shortly before King Louis XVI was executed in January 1793, numerous deputies of the Convention wrote pamphlets or made speeches that were either for or against taking this step. One of the few against, excerpted here, was by C.F.G. Morrison.

In the name of France, hear me out in silence, however shocking some of my reflections may appear. Citizens, like you I am overcome with the greatest indignation when I consider the many crimes, the atrocities, with which Louis XVI is stained. My first and doubtless most natural impulse is to see this bloody monster [be tormented and killed]. Yet I must deny my impulse and heed instead the voice of reason [and] consult the spirit and disposition of our law. . . . The Convention abolished the monarchy. From that moment, Louis had ceased to be king in law. . . . Here, the National Convention . . . has nothing more to decide, since by his de facto deposition [dethronement] he has already undergone the only punishment determined for those crimes which he committed while he was yet king.

Quoted in Michael Walzer, ed., *Regicide and Revolution: Speeches at the Trial of Louis XVI.* trans. Marian Rothstein. Cambridge, England: Cambridge University Press, 1974, pp. 110, 120.

group of dissatisfied Parisian shopkeepers, artisans, and factory workers called the sans-culottes. (The term means "without breeches," a reference to the long trousers working people wore, in contrast to the knee breeches traditionally worn by nobles.) The members of this new coalition were galvanized into radical action partly by the impending threat of the advancing Prussian army. On September 21, 1792, they created a legislative body they called the "Convention" and proclaimed France to be a republic.

Implicit in the definition of the term *republic* was the fact that the monarchy was now outdated and invalid. Moreover, the very presence of the monarch and his royal relatives made the new radical leaders feel uncomfortable, even humiliated. "The king was there," scholars Norah Lofts and Margery Weiner write, "alive in the prison." He was "an anachronism," that is, a relic of the past, and "an embarrassing one."[42]

The radical leaders of the Convention decided, therefore, that getting rid of Louis would be best for all. However, no one was willing to go so far as to kill him without a trial, an act that might turn the people against the Convention. So they proceeded to put the

The King's Last Speech

King Louis XVI delivered his last public speech on December 26, 1792, at the end of his trial. He said in part:

Speaking to you perhaps for the last time, I declare to you that my conscience does not reproach me in any way and that my defenders have told you nothing but the truth. I have never feared a public examination of my conduct. But it wounds my heart to find in the indictment the charge that I wished to shed the people's blood. . . . I confess that the often repeated pledges that I have at all times given of my love for the people and the way in which I have always behaved seem to me an evident proof that I had little fear of endangering myself in order to spare their blood, and that these pledges and this behavior should preserve me forever from any such imputation [accusation].

Quoted in Bernard Fay, *Louis XVI; or, The End of the World*. trans. Patrick O'Brian. Chicago: Henry Regnery, 1968, p. 397.

king on trial in December 1792. "The king made a poor appearance," Lofts and Weiner continue.

Denied the use of a razor for three days, he wore the beginning of a beard on cheeks that now sagged flabbily. His brown coat was shabby. [But] there still clung about him the ghost, the vanishing shadow of royalty. He had been allowed counsel to defend him, [but] against what? For being born to the throne? Being passive? Being stupid? When the prosecution declared, "Louis, the French nation is your accuser," the impersonal nature of the trial was revealed. It was not Louis who was on trial; it was the system of monarchy.[43]

The Girondins, now a minority in the legislature, tried but failed to save the king's life. He was sentenced to death and beheaded in a bloody public spectacle on January 21, 1793. Many of the legislators, along with other French, hoped that the bloodshed was at last over. But they were wrong, for the worst was yet to come.

Chapter Five

Terror in the Name of Liberty

In the months following the execution of Louis XVI, the leaders of the Convention in Paris faced a wide array of problems and threats. These included the ongoing war with neighboring countries, which rapidly expanded in scope and intensity and threatened France with invasion; the plots that the French émigrés continued to hatch against the Revolution; uprisings of rural peasants who did not want to fight in the war; a national economy in shambles because of all the civil and social unrest; and the unpredictable Paris mob, which various political factions might at any moment sway against the Revolution's leaders.

Collectively, many of these leaders felt these difficulties and dangers foreshadowed the Revolution's collapse and France's descent into chaos. The result would be a loss of the liberty and human rights that the Revolution had so far achieved at great cost. The only realistic way to prevent such a catastrophe, the more radical deputies decided, was to crack down on any and all who threatened the ideals and implementation of the Revolutionary government. In a speech to the Convention, Robespierre justified using force to preserve liberty:

It is time to firmly trace the goal of the Revolution [and] to take account of ourselves, [and] of the obstacles that keep us from our goal, and of the means we must adopt to attain it. . . . To what goal do we move? The peaceful enjoyment of liberty and equality. . . . [This can happen only if the government enforces social harmony. So this] representative body must thus begin by subjecting all the private passions it contains to the general passion of public good. [If] the motivating force of popular

France Adopts the Guillotine

Many of the executions carried out during the Revolution utilized the guillotine, a device in which a huge blade falls vertically, slicing off the victim's head. It was named for Joseph-Ignace Guillotin, a Paris doctor who told the Assembly that it would be a swift and painless form of execution for people of all social classes. Similar devices had already been used in England, Scotland, and elsewhere for more than a century. But the Assembly's deputies ordered that a French version be constructed by a German mechanic following a design by Dr. Antoine Louis, then a prominent member of the French College of Physicians. (For this reason, the device was briefly referred to as the "Louisette," after Dr. Louis. The first use of the term *guillotine* was in a Paris journal in April 1792.)

The guillotine was the primary instrument used in performing executions during the Reign of Terror.

Property of Bradley Beach Public Library

government in peacetime is virtue, the motivating force . . . in revolution is both virtue and terror. . . . Terror is nothing other than prompt, stern, inflexible justice. Terror thus issues from virtue. [It is] a consequence of the general principle of democracy applied to the most pressing needs of the fatherland.[44]

In the name of liberty, therefore, Robespierre and his colleagues instituted what came to be known as the "Reign of Terror," often called more simply "the Terror." It lasted from September 1793 to late July 1794. It enforced its authority through a series of revolutionary decrees and tribunals (committees, hearings, and trials) in which "enemies" of the new republic were arrested and in many cases executed. The exact number of victims remains unclear. But at least 300,000 people were arrested and perhaps as many as 20,000 lost their lives. Eventually, this fury of suspicion, deceit, paranoia, and violence could no longer sustain itself. Even its leaders came to be seen as suspects, and as they turned on one another the Terror began to destroy itself.

Maximilien Robespierre and his colleagues instituted what became known as the "Reign of Terror," where as many as twenty thousand people may have lost their lives.

The Coming of the Terror

It is possible that the Reign of Terror would never have occurred if France had been at peace in 1793. However, as that year began the French were already at war with Austria and Prussia (in what posterity came to call the War of the First Coalition). Then, when King Louis was executed on January 21, shocked heads of state across Europe expressed their outrage by expelling their French ambassadors. In response, the Convention in Paris declared war on Britain, Holland, and Spain. Soon revolutionary France stood alone against nearly every major European power. (Other European nations, even the few not at war with France, feared the outbreak of similar rebellions in their own countries. So most of them instituted highly repressive domestic policies. Early in 1793, for example,

British leaders made it possible to commit treason in writing and attempted to censor the press. Also Prussian leaders joined with the aristocracy and Lutheran Church to stifle dissent. In Russia, Queen Catherine burned the works of popular French philosophers, including Voltaire, and exiled freedom-minded Russian writers to Siberia.)

Robespierre, Danton, and the other leaders of the Mountain, who now headed France's government, at first felt confident that France could achieve victory in the war. For one thing, they reasoned, the country had a large population from which to draw soldiers. And they took advantage of that fact when in the summer of 1793 the Convention drafted virtually everyone in France into some sort of military service. "The French people are in permanent requisition for army service," the "Defense of the Republic Levy" stated. "The young men shall go to battle. The married men shall forge arms and transport provisions. The women shall

Jean-Paul Marat's death in 1793 helped to launch the Reign of Terror into full swing.

make tents and clothes and shall serve in the hospitals. The children shall turn old linen into lint [for use in muskets]. . . . National buildings shall be converted into barracks [and] public places into armament workshops."[45]

Another reason that France's revolutionary leaders were certain of victory was their steadfast belief in their cause. They were sure that the French, as champions of human freedom, were destined to prevail over the forces of monarchy and oppression. They expressed this belief by having all French battle banners inscribed with the words: "The French people have risen against tyrants."

In addition to overseeing the national effort to fight the forces of the First Coalition, the Convention's deputies faced an equally daunting task. Namely, they had to govern and stabilize a large nation still filled with opposing political groups and unrest. To confront this challenge, Mountain leaders formed a series of "committees," groups of men charged with individual, targeted goals.

The most important and powerful of these groups, the Committee of Public Safety, rapidly assumed nearly complete governmental authority. Its radical members, especially Robespierre, Danton, Louis-Antoine Saint-Just, and Lazare Carnot, became powerful and widely feared. Another fanatic, the newspaper man Jean-Paul Marat, was not a member of this (or any other) government group; but he agreed with and aided Robespierre and the other members of the Committee. They even profited by Marat's untimely and brutal death. In July 1793 he was fatally stabbed in his bathtub by a young woman who backed the Girondins. The Committee promptly used the incident to discredit the Girondins, who were critical of its activities and tactics.

Among these questionable tactics was the Committee's increasing use of undemocratic decrees, intimidation, and even brutality to achieve its idealistic aims. By September 1793 the Terror and dictatorship were in full swing. "This was not a dictatorship of any one particular member," a modern scholar points out, "but the committee certainly exercised the powers of a dictatorial regime."[46] Robespierre and his accomplices claimed they had no other choice. They faced an extreme national emergency, they said, and the use of force was the only means of restoring stability and safety. After this restoration, they promised, there would no longer be any need for suppressive measures. One popular Parisian newspaper accepted this argument and tried to sell it to its readers. "Yes, terror is the order of the day, and ought to be," an editorial began.

Is not the French Revolution [a battle] to the death between those who want to be free and those content to be slaves? This is the situation, and the French people have gone too far to retreat with honor and safety. There is no middle ground. France must be utterly free or perish in the attempt, and any means are justifiable in fighting for so fine a cause. But our resources are being exhausted, say some. Well, when the Revolution is finished, they will be replenished by peace.[47]

The Tools of Suppression

The radical, ruthless men who now ran France needed powerful, effective tools to maintain and assert their dictatorial authority. One of these tools was the secretive, autocratic (having unlimited authority) structure and powers of the Committee of Public Safety itself. A decree issued in April 1793 outlined these powers:

This committee shall deliberate in secret. It shall be responsible for supervising and accelerating the work of [the revolutionary government], whose decrees it may even suspend when it believes them contrary to the national interest. . . . It is authorized to take, in urgent circumstances, measures for general defense, both internal and external, and its decrees . . . shall be executed without delay.[48]

Thus, when Robespierre and his fellow petty dictators felt that a decree passed by the Convention was "contrary to the national interest," they could veto it. This was completely contrary to democratic principles. As in all dictatorships in recorded history, the "national interest" inevitably could not be separated from the personal interests of the dictators themselves.

Of course, the Committee's members justified their assumption of these powers by citing national security concerns. National security also became the excuse for the creation of a means for identifying the government's (and often the dictators') enemies. It took the form of the "Law of Suspects," passed in September 1793, which read in part:

The following are deemed suspected persons: those who, by their conduct, associations, talk, or writings have shown themselves partisans of tyranny or federalism and enemies of liberty . . . those to whom certificates of patriotism have been refused . . . those former nobles, husbands, wives, fathers, mothers, sons or daughters . . . and agents of the *émigrés*, who have not steadily manifested their devotion to the Revolution.[49]

Later, even more repressive measures were enacted, widening the net in which the tyrannical members of the Committee hoped to ensnare their enemies. The most dictatorial of all was the "Law of 22 Prairial Year II," passed on June 10, 1794. "The revolutionary tribunal is instituted in order to punish the enemies of the people," one article stated.

The enemies of the people are those who seek to destroy public liberty . . . [those] who have [tried] to depreciate [criticize] the National Convention . . . those who have deceived the people or the represen-

The revolutionary tribunal meets to hear the testimony of a family on trial during the French Revolution.

tatives of the people in order to lead them into operations contrary to the interests of liberty . . . those who have spread false news in order to divide and disturb the people . . . those who have sought to [corrupt the public's morals] and conscience [and] the purity of the revolutionary principles.

The law also spelled out the punishment that awaited these enemies. "Every citizen has the right to seize conspirators and counter-revolutionaries and to arraign them before magis-

trates. He is required to denounce them when he knows of them. . . . The accused shall be examined in public session. . . . The penalty provided for all offenses, the jurisdiction [authority] of which belongs to the revolutionary tribunal, is death."[50]

A Systematic and Pitiless Slaughter

These revolutionary documents demonstrate how the definition of an "enemy" of the people swiftly expanded, making more and more people and groups

Queen Marie-Antoinette replies to charges brought against her during a trial in which she was found guilty and sentenced to death.

suspect. Based on such suspicions, those in power proceeded to run amok. Having been empowered by the Committee's obsessive decrees, they engaged in a systematic, at times enthusiastic, often pitiless, and mostly needless slaughter of thousands of people. In Christopher Hibbert's words:

> Whole families were led to the scaffold for no other crime than their relationship; sisters for shedding tears over the death of their brothers in the emigrant armies; wives for lamenting the fate of their husbands. . . . Others were sentenced on the strength of denunciations by jealous or vindictive neighbors. One victim was fetched from prison to face a charge which had been brought against another prisoner with a similar name. Her protests were silenced by the prosecutor, who said casually, "Since she's here, we might just as well take her."[51]

The most famous of the Terror's victims were the former queen, Marie-Antoinette, members of the royal family, and several other nobles. The queen had already suffered greatly from the loss of her husband, her royal status, and her once luxurious lifestyle. But this was not enough for the extremists now running the government. She was arrested, charged with treason and committing incest with her son, and held in a cell in the Conciergerie, a prison near Notre Dame Cathedral in Paris.

Marie-Antoinette's trial took place on October 14, 1793. When called to comment on the incest charge, which was almost certainly false, she replied: "If I give no answer, it is because nature itself refuses to accept such an accusation brought against a mother. I appeal to all the mothers here present."[52] These words elicited some sympathy from the spectators. Nevertheless, the judge threatened to clear the court and speeded up the inevitable process of finding her guilty. Denied any right to appeal, she was executed two days later (October 16) in the same manner as her husband—beheaded in public by a guillotine.

Former aristocrats and suspected counterrevolutionaries were not the only victims of the Terror. As time went

The Queen in Prison

One of Marie-Antoinette's lawyers later recalled her situation in prison just prior to her trial:

On October 14th, 1793, I happened to be in the country when I received the news that I had been named . . . to defend the Queen before the revolutionary tribunal. . . . I immediately set out for the prison filled with a sense of the sacred duty. . . . After passing through two gates one enters a dark corridor. . . . On the right are the cells, and on the left there is a chamber into which the light enters by two small barred windows looking onto the little courtyard reserved for women. It was in this chamber that the Queen was confined. It was divided into two parts by a screen. On the left . . . was an armed [guard], and on the right the part of the room occupied by the Queen containing a bed, a table and two chairs. Her Majesty was attired in a white dress of extreme simplicity. . . . In presenting myself to the Queen with respectful devotion, I felt my knees trembling under me and my eyes wet with tears.

Quoted in Georges Pernoud and Sabine Flaissier, eds., *The French Revolution*. trans. Richard Graves. New York: Capricorn, 1961, pp. 203–204.

on, its administrators became both suspicious and bold enough to eliminate fellow revolutionaries and Convention deputies. Some were targeted for being too moderate. These included several Girondins who had urged the ruling group to use more caution and humanity. Others were arrested on false charges simply because Robespierre and his colleagues on the Committee did not like or trust them.

The End of the Terror

Such injustices, which many viewed as a disgrace to the Revolution's original ideals, continued with increasing intensity until they ended in a shocking spectacle. Simply put, the Terror's principal leaders began to kill their own. Danton was the first to go. He had begun to see that many of the recent arrests had been unreasonable and had the nerve to say so in a speech delivered to the Convention in late January 1794. "No one asked for revolutionary committees more than I," he declared. "They were necessary then. [However, we must] be wary. . . . Justice must be rendered in such a way that it will not weaken the strictness of our measures."[53]

Terror to Safeguard Liberty

On September 5, 1793, the Convention in Paris voted in favor of the idea of using "terror," or necessary force, to destroy all enemies of the Revolution, be they real or potential. One deputy told those gathered:

Legislators, it is time to put an end to the impious struggle that has been going on since 1789 between the sons and daughters of the nation and those who have abandoned it. Your fate, and ours, is tied to the unvarying establishment of the republic. We must either destroy its enemies, or they will destroy us. They have thrown down the gauntlet in the midst of the People, who have picked it up. They have stirred up agitation. They have attempted to separate, to divide the mass of the citizens, in order to crush the People and to avoid being crushed themselves. Today, the mass of the People, who are without resources, must destroy them using their own weight and willpower. . . . Let us crush the enemies of the revolution, and starting today, let the government take action, let the laws be executed, let the lot of the People be strengthened, and let liberty be saved.

Quoted in "Terror Is the Order of the Day," Liberty, Equality, Fraternity: Exploring the French Revolution (http://chnm.gmu.edu/revolution/d/416/).

For expressing such sentiments, Danton was arrested on March 30. After enduring a farcical trial with a predetermined outcome, he and another revolutionary seen as too moderate, Camille Desmoulins, were guillotined on April 5. Reportedly, Danton's last words were: "Show my head to the people. It is worth seeing."[54]

It soon became clear to most other members of the Convention that, if Danton was not safe, no one was. But eventually, the moderates gathered enough courage to challenge Robespierre and the remaining dictators. On July 27, 1794, cries of "Down with the tyrant!"[55] echoed through the hall as they publicly condemned him. They also denounced Saint-Just. The next day these two men and nineteen of their closest supporters felt the executioner's blade. For these overzealous revolutionaries, the wheel of justice had come full circle. Though the Reign of Terror was over, the larger Revolution had not yet expended its considerable energies.

Chapter Six

Changes in French Society and Culture

During the first four to five years of the French Revolution, French society and culture underwent a series of distinct changes. Almost all of these were seen as progressive and enlightened at the time, at least by the leaders and supporters of the Revolution. In their view society—including various basic social institutions and customs—needed to keep pace with politics. The main principles of political change wrought by these revolutionaries were human equality and freedom and the rights of individual citizens to control their government. It seemed only natural and correct that these same ideas should be applied to society, too. Thus, the various revolutionary assemblies pushed to rid society of those institutions and customs that denied or discouraged individual freedom of expression and a person's right to determine his or her own destiny.

For example, the Catholic Church had long been one of the most powerful institutions in France. Its bishops and priests controlled many aspects of French society, life, and thought, including education and marriage customs. The Revolution's leaders felt that the Church had too much control over society and that it discouraged individual thought and expression. So they swiftly moved to place the churches under government control and to limit the powers and privileges of the clergy. At one point, the most radical revolutionaries even attempted to replace traditional religious beliefs with state-sponsored secular (nonreligious) beliefs.

Similarly, the state took over the Church's role in education by establishing public schools. Marriage customs were overhauled, and divorce was legalized. Also a new calendar was introduced, along with new secular holidays. In addition the revolutionaries established a national institute of arts and sciences and a new system of weights and measures.

Some of these innovations and changes did not survive very long following the end of the Revolution. Also the revolutionaries were not progressive enough in certain social areas; despite their idealism about equality, for instance, they refused to grant women the same political rights men enjoyed. Nevertheless, the Revolution had profound effects on French society and thought and in many ways paved the way for the emergence of modern secular French and European culture.

The New Calendar

The French revolutionaries wanted to wipe out as many bad memories of the nation's past as they could, including the calendar and holidays that had been established by the Church and kings. In October 1793 the members of a committee chosen to draw up a new calendar reported:

The main idea upon which we have based our proposal is to use the calendar to consecrate the agricultural system, to lead the nation back to it, highlighting periods and times of the year with clear or tangible signs taken from agriculture and the rural economy. . . . We have therefore developed the idea of giving each month of the year a characteristic name that depicts its unique temperature and the types of agricultural produce in season at that time. . . . Thus the [new] names of the months are:

AUTUMN
Vendémiaire (Vintage)
Brumaire (Fog)
Frimaire (Frost)

WINTER
Nivôse (Snow)
Pluviôse (Rain)
Ventôse (Wind)

SPRING
Germinal (Buds)
Floréal (Flowers)
Prairial (Meadow)

SUMMER
Messidor (Harvest)
Thermidor (Heat)
Fructidor (Fruit)

Quoted in "The Calendar," Liberty, Equality, Fraternity: Exploring the French Revolution (http://chnm.gmu.edu/revolution/d/435/).

Attempts to Reform Religion

Religious developments in France constitute a clear example of how the Revolution permanently altered the country's society and culture. The revolutionaries assaulted the Catholic Church for a number of reasons. First, they felt it was unfair that the bishops had special privileges and treated the commoners as inferiors. Among these privileges was exemption from paying taxes, which all commoners had to pay. Another religious custom the revolutionaries viewed as an abuse was the tithe. This was a proportion of each commoner's yearly income that he or she had to pay to help support the Church. Many French also resented the high levels of corruption that existed among the bishops and the fact that the bishops always sided with the nobles against the commoners. "The 'good conscience' of 1789 wanted the Church to be purer [and] poorer," scholar Emmet Kennedy points out, "more responsive to the indigent [needy] and

French Catholics attend a secret mass during the Reign of Terror.

more removed from the [royal] court and aristocracy."[56]

The first assaults on the Church came in the Revolution's opening months. Among the feudal privileges the National Assembly abolished on August 4, 1789, was the tithe. This was a serious blow to the bishops, who had long counted on the tithe as one of their principal sources of income. The Assembly struck the Church an even harsher blow on November 2. By a vote of 568 to 346, the deputies agreed to confiscate the vast lands owned by the clergy and place them at the disposal of the French people. The Church's authority was also undermined by Article 10 of the new *Declaration of Rights*, which lessened the clergy's strong influence over the way people thought and expressed themselves. "No one should be disturbed on account of his opinion, even religious [opinion],"[57] the article states.

These controversial moves proved to be only the start of more comprehensive ones in which the Assembly made the Church nothing more than a part of the state and thereby subject to state rules. In July 1790 the deputies passed the "Civil Constitution of the Clergy." It ordained that clergymen's salaries be paid by the state; reduced the number of parishes; matched up each diocese (church district) with one of the new geographic departments the Assembly had recently created; and most controversial of all, mandated that priests and bishops be chosen by the people in free elections (rather than by church offi-

cials). Even more humiliating for clergymen was the demand that they recite an oath of loyalty to the state, as follows: "I swear to be faithful to the nation, to the law and the king, and to maintain with all my power the Constitution determined by the National Assembly and accepted by the king."[58]

The Cult of the Supreme Being

An even more vigorous assault on the Church came in late 1793 and early 1794 at the hands of the radical leaders of the committees enforcing the Terror. The goal was literally to de-Christianize France. As Christopher Hibbert tells it:

Religious monuments outside churches were destroyed. Various religious ceremonies were suppressed. . . . Not only streets and squares but towns and villages [changed from religious to secular] names. The bestowal on babies of revolutionary first names became more common in certain districts than those of saints. More and more cathedrals and churches were deprived of their ornaments, vessels, and [gold] plate [and] some were converted into Temples of Reason. [Also] many clergy resigned and a number married.[59]

In place of Christianity, the extremists tried to establish the "Cult of the Supreme Being." That being, a deist god like the one envisioned by Thomas Jefferson and several other American founding fathers, supposedly created

The Festival of the Supreme Being was founded by Robespierre in 1794 in an attempt to replace Christianity in France.

the universe but thereafter did not intervene in human affairs. In the summer of 1794, Robespierre founded the annual Festival of the Supreme Being, saying in part:

The eternally happy day which the French people consecrate to the Supreme Being has finally arrived. Never has the world he created offered him a sight so worthy of his eyes. He has seen tyranny, crime, and deception reign on earth. At this moment, he sees an entire nation, at war with all the oppressors of the human race, suspend its heroic efforts in order to raise its thoughts and vows to the Great Being who gave it the mission to undertake these efforts and the strength to execute them.[60]

Not surprisingly, angry Catholic reactions soon set in against the various attacks on the Church. In March 1791 the pope in Rome condemned these assaults. Many French, faced with choosing between patriotism and religious conviction, found themselves in a crisis of conscience. Tens of thousands of them demanded that their churches be reopened and that decorations and other church items that had been removed be returned. Some people even worried that various local natural disasters that occurred each year might be God's punishment for the Revolution's antireligious policies.

Christianity was too ingrained in French society to be eradicated by a few government edicts and programs. As a result, in the years following the revolutionary era, the Catholic Church rebounded. Still, it recovered only a fraction of the power and influence it had possessed before the Revolution. Having been humbled in the people's eyes, thereafter the clergy was obliged to cater more to the needs of its church members.

Educational Developments

Reorganizing the Church necessarily resulted in other reforms, among them a new school system. Before the French Revolution, education had been primarily in the hands of the clergy. Classes were held mainly in parish halls, taught by priests, restricted to children of the upper and middle classes, and paid for by the students' parents. The Enlightenment concepts that had inspired the Revolution (such as equality and democratic principles) were largely excluded from the curriculum.

In securalizing church activities the revolutionaries dismantled the old schools. The new system they created featured both primary and secondary (higher) education regulated by the government and open to all children, an approach later adopted in all modern Western societies. The Jacobins and other revolutionaries saw two major goals of the new schools. First, they would give young citizens basic skills that would give them all an equal chance in life; second, they would indoctrinate children in the Revolution's ideals, thereby helping to continue the new, fairer revolutionary society. In a

French intellectual Marie-Jean de Condorcet said that France's new educational system should be open to all children.

The New Metric System

Among the many cultural changes initiated by the revolutionaries was the introduction of the metric system for weights and measures, which was simpler and more uniform than the many conflicting systems that then existed in Europe. An April 1795 decree stated in part:

There is only one standard of weights and measures for the entire Republic; there shall be a platinum ruler on which will be marked the *meter*, which has been adopted as the fundamental unit of the whole system of measurement. . . . Henceforth the new measures shall be [called]:

> *Meter*, the measure equal to one-ten millionth of the arc of the terrestrial meridian included between the north pole and the equator; *Acre*, The measure of area for land, equal to a square, ten meters to a side. . . . *Liter*, the measure of volume, both for liquids and for dry material, the capacity of which shall be the cube of one-tenth of a meter; *Gram*, the absolute weight of a volume of pure water equal to the cube of one one-hundredth of a meter, at the temperature of melting ice. Finally the monetary unit shall take the name of [the] *franc*.

Quoted in John H. Stewart, ed., *A Documentary Survey of the French Revolution*. New York: Macmillan, 1971, pp. 555–56.

report to the legislators, noted French intellectual Marie-Jean de Condorcet summarized the new system's ambitious aims this way: "Education must be universal [and] extend to all citizens. [Also] it must, in its several degrees, comprise the entire system of human knowledge, and assure to men of all ages the facility of preserving their knowledge or of acquiring new knowledge."[61]

To these ends, in 1794 the Convention enacted a system of primary schools for all French boys and girls. The legislation read in part:

The primary schools shall be distributed throughout the territory of the Republic in proportion to population; accordingly, there shall be one primary school for every 1,000 inhabitants. . . . Each primary school shall be divided into two sections, one for boys and one for girls; accordingly, there shall be one man teacher and one woman teacher. . . . The teachers shall be chosen by the people; nevertheless, throughout the duration of the Revolutionary Government, they shall be examined, selected, and supervised by a jury of instruction composed of three [local government officials].[62]

In addition to their selection by the people, the teachers were paid by the state. The state also mandated the curriculum, which included instruction in reading and writing; the new *Declaration of Rights* and Constitution; morality (as defined by the revolutionaries); French language; geography and natural phenomena (science); heroic national songs; and daily physical exercise.

The Convention also set up secondary schools, equivalent to modern high schools. There was a "central school" located in each of the new departments. In addition the government established college-like institutions that included a school of public works (which in the twentieth century became one of the finest technical schools in the world); an early version of a teachers' college; three medical colleges; and the National Institute, which offered classes in science, mathematics, philosophy, literature, and the arts.

Women's Roles

Education turned out to be the main area of advancement for French women during the Revolution. The vast majority of men, including the radical revolutionaries, and most women too, accepted traditional views of women and their societal roles. Both before and during the Revolution, many French women worked as farmers, laundresses, and shopkeepers. Most, however, were also wives and mothers, which they felt were their chief roles. The ideal woman was summarized by a Jacobin journalist, who gave this advice in 1793:

"Be honest and diligent girls, tender and modest wives, wise mothers, and you will be good patriots. True patriotism consists of fulfilling one's duties and valuing only rights appropriate to each according to sex and age, and not wearing the [liberty] cap [and] not carrying pike and pistol. Leave those to men who are born to protect you and make you happy."[63]

This is not to say that women did not play important roles in the Revolution, for they did. Groups of women often demonstrated in the streets or rioted over bread prices. Their dramatic march on Versailles on October 5, 1789, was a noteworthy example. But in large degree such activities were only extensions of traditional women's social roles and activities. Women had long been "purchasers of and negotiators for bread in the marketplace," English scholar Olwen Hufton points out. "Not only were they sensitive to prices, but they had a special role to play in defense of the consumer interests of the family. . . . Women believed themselves invested with specific (and never defined) powers to riot [to promote those interests] without incurring legal action if certain rules [such as not destroying anyone's property] were respected."[64]

Women played a significant role during the French Revolution by demonstrating over issues such as bread prices.

Some women, especially in Paris, also joined women's clubs, which were a novelty during the Revolution. But most of these organizations did not discuss or promote the acquisition of political rights for women, then seen as an extremely radical notion.

Only a handful of women and men lobbied for such rights. Among them was Condorcet, who in 1790 helped establish the Social Circle, a group that campaigned for female equality. The most daring advocate of women's rights during the Revolution was Marie Gouze, better known by her pen name, Olympe de Gouges. In September 1791 she published *The Declaration of Rights of Women*, which stated in part:

Woman is born free and remains equal to man in rights. . . . The law should be the expression of the general will. All citizenesses and citizens should take part, in person or by their representatives, in its formation. It must be the same for everyone. All citizenesses and citizens, being equal in its eyes, should be equally admissible to all public dignities, offices and employments, according to their ability, and with no other distinction than that of their virtues and talents.[65]

Such efforts to advance women's political rights did not garner much

How Society Viewed Women

One of the major literary works of the European Enlightenment, The Encyclopedia *(edited by leading intellectual Denis Diderot and published between 1751 and 1772), included the following information in its article about women, reflecting the thinking of that time.*

Even though husband and wife have the same fundamental interests in society, it is nevertheless essential that governmental authority rests with either one or the other. The positive rights of civilized nations, like the laws and customs of Europe, now grant this authority unanimously and definitively to the male, who, being gifted with greater strength of mind and body, contributes more to the common good in matters both human and holy. Women then, must necessarily be subordinate to their husbands and obey his orders on all household issues. These are the opinions of legal advisors, both in olden times and now, as well as the unequivocal decision of legislators.

Quoted in "Article from the *Encyclopedia:* 'Woman'," Liberty, Equality, Fraternity: Exploring the French Revolution (http://chnm.gmu.edu/revolution/d/469/).

support. And French women did not obtain these rights until much later (1944). But it was in the 1790s, during the Revolution, that they at least began to awaken to the realization that they were in many ways equal to men and might someday enjoy equality under the law.

Marriage and Divorce

One social realm that underwent change to the benefit of women was that of marriage and divorce. The revolutionary deputies strongly felt that marriage should be taken out of the clergy's hands. "By secularizing marriage," Lynn Hunt writes, "the state gained control over the civil registers (births, deaths, marriages) and replaced the Church as the ultimate authority in questions of family life."[66] Thus, the new government decreed that henceforth marriages must be performed by a local government official. (If the bride and groom desired it, a priest could witness the ceremony.)

During the French Revolution marriages were no longer performed by clergy, but instead by local government officials.

A more sweeping change was the legalization of divorce, which previously had not been allowed. As for the grounds, either a man or a woman could now seek a divorce if the spouse was insane, committed a major crime, beat his or her partner, repeatedly engaged in immoral acts, abandoned his or her partner for two years or more, or engaged in counterrevolutionary activities. In addition, by mutual consent a husband and wife could claim they were incompatible and divorce after a six-month waiting period. Finally, all divorced persons were required to wait a year before remarrying. At the time, this was by far the most liberal divorce law in the world, one of many ways the Revolution had wrought radical changes in French society.

Chapter Seven

Napoléon and the Revolution's End

The execution of Robespierre and several of his accomplices and supporters brought the Terror to a crashing halt. Most of the legislators in the Convention realized that the Revolution had grown far too radical and that it was time for the revolutionaries to reassess their situation. As they did so, one of the more prominent and respected of their number, Pierre-Toussaint Duran-Maillane, made a speech calling for moderation, which he summed up later in this passage from his memoirs:

My speech, which was nothing more than a motion calling for the freedom of opinion, was delivered on [August 21, 1794], a little more than three weeks after the fall of Robespierre. [I] reminded [my fellow deputies] how unjust a persecution is that can lead to the gallows simply for having an

opinion. This reprimand was taken to heart. . . . Every honest man should want that the freedom of opinion never be jeopardized by unproven charges or invective [scorn]. We should not swear at men whom we look upon as "weak beings" in order to shackle the opinions that they only want to express for the good of the People. If someone here believes that they should make a serious reproach toward one of his colleagues, let him explain himself and stipulate the facts, not just offer insults. Let the accused be heard, and let us not seek to make people fear from threats.[67]

The vast majority of the deputies agreed with these words. And as a result, there now ensued a generally more moderate phase of the Revolution —the so-called "Thermidorian Reaction." The term *Thermidorian* was derived from Thermidor, the name given to the period of late July and early August in the new revolutionary calendar (introduced by the Convention in September 1793). Accordingly, in the years directly following the end of the Terror, government officials were often referred to as Thermidorians.

The Thermidorians first busied themselves with dismantling most of the laws and tribunals created during the Terror. They also freed those deputies whom the extremists had imprisoned and allowed them to retake their seats in the Convention. Then the legislators turned their attention to the government itself. Clearly, they concluded, the constitution they had created a few years before had proved inadequate to the country's needs. So they must construct a new constitution.

Robespierre lies on a table after shooting himself. The former French Revolution leader had tried to kill himself before being arrested and executed.

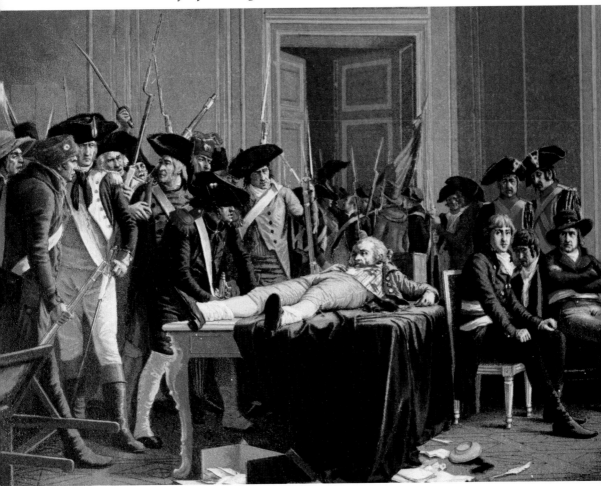

The fruit of their labors, introduced in August 1795, made France a sort of modified republic that can better be described as an oligarchy. From ancient Greek words meaning "rule of the few," an oligarchy is a government in which a relatively small number of individuals share authority, each providing a check on the powers of the others. But though this approach was well meaning, time would prove it ineffective. The new leaders did such a good job of limiting their powers that they were unable to counter the steady rise of power in another quarter—the army. It would be a strong and irresistible military general who would eventually galvanize and stabilize the nation, finally bringing the Revolution to an end.

Establishment of the Directory

The government ushered in by the new Constitution acquired the general name "the Directory," after one of its branches. It was intended to be a parliamentary system in which power would be shared between a legislative branch and an executive branch. To help avoid the kind of abuses that had occurred under the Convention, the legislature was divided into two houses, each of which could check the powers of the other. One house, the Council of Five Hundred (with five hundred members, as the name suggests), was given the authority to enact new laws. The other house, the Council of Ancients, had 250 members, each of whom had to be at least forty years old. They could not make laws; but they could veto any laws made by the other house.

The executive branch, the Directory, consisted of five men of equal status and authority. They were chosen by the Ancients from among the ranks of the Five Hundred. To help keep a single executive from amassing too much power, one of the five men was required to retire each year, so that the longest any one director could serve was five years.

The Constitution of 1795 also put new limits on the people's voting rights in an attempt to make voters more responsible and discourage mob mentality and violence. For example, only citizens with a certain amount of property, along with all soldiers, were permitted to vote for members of the two legislative houses. Also, as the following constitutional provisions indicate, certain restraints were placed on the rights to assemble and redress grievances:

No private society [group] which concerns itself with political questions may correspond with another, or affiliate therewith, or hold public sessions composed of the members of the societies and of associates distinguished from one another, or impose conditions of admission and eligibility, or arrogate [claim] to itself rights of exclusion, or cause its members to wear any external insignia of their association. . . . Citizens may exercise their political rights only in the primary or communal assem-

Rules for Selecting the Directors

The French Constitution of 1795 spelled out the political structure of the Directory. About the five directors making up the executive branch, it stated:

The Executive Power shall be delegated to a Directory of five members appointed by the Legislative Body. . . . The Council of Five-Hundred shall prepare, by secret ballot, a list of [fifty potential] members of the Directory to be appointed, and shall present it to the Council of Ancients, which shall choose, also by secret ballot, from said list. The members of the Directory must be at least forty years of age. They may be chosen only from among citizens who have been ministers or members of the Legislative Body. . . . The Directory shall be renewed in part by the election of one new member annually. During the first four years, the order of retirement of those first elected shall be determined by lot. None of the retiring members may be reelected until after an interval of five years. Ancestors and descendants in direct line, brothers, uncles and nephews, first cousins, and those related by marriage . . . may not be members of the Directory at one and the same time.

Quoted in "Constitution of the Year III (1795)," Liberty, Equality, Fraternity: Exploring the French Revolution (http://chnm.gmu.edu/revolution/d/450/).

blies. . . . All citizens shall be free to address petitions to the public authorities, but they must be individual ones; no association may present them collectively, except the constituted authorities, and only for matters within their competence. The petitioners must never forget the respect due the constituted authorities.[68]

The Military's Increasing Role

The Directory appeared to be more or less adequate to the task of governing France, at least for the moment. However, the legislators and directors were totally inadequate to the job of fighting the foreign war that still raged outside the country's borders. Fortunately for the French, the tide in that conflict had turned, mostly in France's favor, in the recent past. French armies had overrun Belgium and annexed its territories to northern France; the Dutch had surrendered; and both Prussia and Spain had made peace with the French. Thus, in the closing weeks of 1795, Austria and Britain were the last major European powers still at war with France.

A meeting of the Directory, the new government established in France by the Constitution of 1795.

Still, the Austrians and British were extremely formidable foes who could potentially defeat the French on their own. So the Directory had to take the ongoing war seriously and try to achieve either victory or a negotiated peace favorable to France. To accomplish such goals, the national leaders in Paris had no choice but to rely on the power of the army, including both the generals and soldiers under their command. But this reliance came at a large price, as the military became increas-

ingly powerful and the government, in turn, more and more dependent on its good will. As scholar Donald Kagan puts it, "The growing role of the [French revolutionary] army held profound consequences not only for France but for the entire world."[69]

The newfound power of the French troops derived partly from the fact that each and every one of them could vote (while many French citizens too poor to own property could not). Collectively speaking, therefore, the soldiers made up a powerful part of the national electorate. Also, and more ominously, most of the troops were no longer animated by the fiery revolutionary zeal they had exhibited in the Revolution's first couple of years. Increasingly, they felt more allegiance to their generals in the field than to the Revolution's leaders in faraway Paris. "The tradition of antagonism towards king, priests, and nobles, was still strong" among the soldiers, Christopher Hibbert points out. "But spirits in the ranks were no longer kept up by enthusiasm for the republican cause. [The troops] felt pride in their regiments and in French might rather than in the Revolution. It was their generals they looked to for leadership now, not the civilians at home."[70]

As for these generals, many were young, ambitious, and eager both to prove themselves in battle and to become powerful national figures. According to Australian scholar Martyn Lyons:

> The republican army offered rapid promotion to talented and ambitious individuals. Deaths, emigration, and dismissals opened up new avenues for social advancement. Many soldiers . . . rose to high positions at a comparatively young age. . . . [Louis-Lazare] Hoche, for example, son of a [mule keeper], was a general at the age of twenty six, and [Pierre-Francois] Augereau, son of a [fruit vendor], emerged from humble origins to become a general in his thirties.[71]

Although the leaders of the Directory worried about the growing power of the generals, they felt that in the long run they would be able to contain that power in the name of the Revolution. But this proved to be a grave error.

Napoléon in Italy

The first major sign of the Directory's underestimation of the threat the military posed came during the military campaigns of 1796–1797. French leaders felt that the most logical and efficient way to defeat the Austrians was to attack them on two major fronts. The first would consist of a thrust at Austria's capital, Vienna, from Germany. The other assault would come from the south, mainly Italy. At the time, Italy was not a united nation, as it is today. Instead, it was a patchwork of small states, some independent, others controlled by various European powers, including Austria. One of the French generals, Napoléon Bonaparte (1769–1821), presented the Directory with a plan for swiftly conquering a large portion of Italy. It would, he argued, put France in an excellent position to go forward with its attack on Austria.

Napoléon, as he is most often called today, was a brilliant, ambitious individual who had been born on the Mediterranean island of Corsica, a French territory. As a young man he had trained as an artillery officer. Later, with the Revolution in full swing, he had supported the Jacobins and become a close associate of Robespierre. In October 1795 Napoléon commanded a force of government troops who put down a group of counterrevolutionaries in Paris, an episode that made him both famous and a hero of the Revolution.

Now a general, and with the consent of the Directory, in March 1796 Napoléon took charge of fifty thousand French troops and headed for Italy. On March 27 he told his men:

Soldiers, you are naked, ill fed! The Government owes you much; it can give you nothing. Your patience, the courage you display in

Napoléon salutes to wounded troops during the Italian campaign beginning in 1796, where he won large sections of Italian land for France.

the midst of these rocks, are admirable; but they procure you no glory, [and] no fame is reflected upon you. I seek to lead you into the most fertile plains in the world. Rich provinces, great cities will be in your power. There you will find honor, glory, and riches.[72]

The troops soon found Napoléon a man of his word as well as a gifted military strategist. He led them to a series of stunning victories that secured large sections of Italy for France. Also, and crucially, he boldly took the initiative and conducted what amounted to his own personal foreign policy, negotiating with the enemy without consulting his bosses in the Directory. For example, he concluded a treaty with Austria in the fall of 1797, which resulted in that nation making peace and dropping out of the war. Soon afterward, he brought all of Italy and Switzerland under French domination.

These events had significant consequences both for Napoléon himself and for the leaders of the French government. "The Italian campaign," in Lyons's words, "did not only make Bonaparte an illustrious commander, it also transformed him into a figure of political importance in European affairs."[73] Also, the members of the Directory, still a weak and indecisive body, now found themselves in an unexpected and very awkward position. But they did not like having a general who exercised so much independent authority. They could not afford to openly oppose a winning commander of such high stature. The Directory "could not argue with a general who delivered such spectacular victories and war booty," Lyons points out. So "they reluctantly accepted his decisions." Napoléon was now "a continental military statesman as well as a military commander and, for him, this constituted a double victory—that of the French over the Austrians, and that of Bonaparte over the civilian government."[74]

Formation of the Consulate

In the two years that followed, Napoléon proceeded to increase his power and reputation even further. He wanted to strike at the British as hard as possible and decided that the most effective way would be to invade Egypt. It was through that country, then a province of the Ottoman Turkish Empire, that products from Britain's most lucrative colony, India, moved (via the Red Sea, then briefly overland to the Mediterranean) into Europe. Napoléon went ahead with the Egyptian expedition early in 1798. He soon lost most of his fleet to British warships. Nevertheless, his army was successful on land, and he began exploiting the country, once again acting mainly on his own initiative.

Most other Europeans were alarmed at the French invasion of Egypt. In response in December 1798 Britain, Austria, Russia, Portugal, and Turkey formed a new anti-French alliance, the so-called Second Coalition. Not long before, a priest-led uprising had broken out in French-ruled Belgium. And in Paris the already fragile and widely

The French Revolution came to an end when Napoléon became the "First Consul," essentially making himself dictator of the country.

unpopular Directory was now confronted with more problems than it could handle.

The opportunistic Napoléon wasted no time in taking advantage of the Directory's weakness. He agreed to play a major role in a military coup (over-throw) against the government. Engineering the plot with him were the former revolutionary Abbé Sieyès, who by that time had risen to become one of the Directory's five members; another director, Charles Maurice de Talleyrand; and Napoléon's bother,

Lucien, leader of the Council of Five Hundred.

The new government came to be known as the Consulate, based on the title Consul, the name of the administrator-generals of the ancient Roman Republic. Three consuls would rule as France's chief executives and serve ten-year terms. Legislation would be created by three citizen assemblies. At first, Sieyès thought he would be the controlling member of the Consulate. But Napoléon assumed that coveted role by drafting a new constitution and, over the course of several months, manipulating both people and laws to attain the position of "First Consul," essentially dictator of France.

This series of events ended the French Revolution. In the course of a decade, France had undergone a tumultuous series of transformations. It had evolved from monarchy to constitutional monarchy, then to constitutional republic, to near anarchy (lawlessness), to oligarchy, and finally to military dictatorship. Napoléon himself delivered the Revolution's obituary, stating on December 15, 1799:

Frenchmen! A constitution is presented to you. It terminates the

The Coup of November 1799

Several years after his eventual fall from power, Napoléon recalled in his memoirs some of the events of the coup that had brought him that power on November 10, 1799.

[I] entered the Council of Ancients and placed [myself] at the bar, opposite to the president. "You stand," [I] said, "upon a volcano. The Republic no longer possesses a government. The Directory is dissolved. Factions are at work. The hour of decision has come. You have called in my arm, and the arms of my comrades to the support of your wisdom. . . . I desire nothing but the safety of the Republic!". . . The force of this speech, and [my] energy, brought over three-quarters of the members of the Council, who rose to indicate their [approval]. . . . [I then went to the Council of Five Hundred, where at first the deputies] rose, crying, "Death to the Dictator!". . . The drum put an end to the clamor. [My] soldiers entered the chamber [with their] bayonets [raised]. The deputies leaped out the windows and dispersed, leaving their gowns, caps, etc. In one moment, the chamber was empty.

Quoted in Napoléon Bonaparte, *Memoirs of the History of France During the Reign of Napoléon, Dictated by the Emperor*, Vol. 1. London: Henry Colburn, 1823, pp. 93-98.

Censorship Replaced Freedom of the Press

After taking power in France, Napoléon, counteracting the spirit of the freedom of the press the revolutionaries had fought for, introduced press censorship to help him maintain control of and reshape pubic opinion. In July 1801 he wrote to one of his secretaries, saying:

Citizen Ripault is to see that he is supplied every day with all the papers that come out. . . . He will read them carefully, make an abstract [summary] of everything they contain likely to influence public opinion, especially with regard to religion, philosophy, and political opinion. He will send me this abstract daily between five and six o'clock [a.m.]. Once every ten days he will send me an analysis of all the books or pamphlets which have appeared during that period, calling attention to any passages on moral questions.

Quoted in Leon Bernard and Theodore B. Hodges, eds., *Readings in European History*. New York: Macmillan, 1958, p. 350.

uncertainties which the provisional government had [recently] introduced. . . . The Constitution is founded on the true principles of representative government, on the sacred rights of property, equality, and liberty. . . . Citizens, the Revolution is established upon the principles which began it. It is ended.[75]

Napoléon presented the war-weary French people with what appeared to be security and order. For the moment, most of them were willing to accept the offer. None among them then foresaw that in the next several years he would lead them to the very brink of European supremacy, but then, regrettably, into disaster's dark depths.

The Revolution's Formidable Legacy

When Napoléon declared in 1799 that the French Revolution was over, he was only partly right. True, the revolutionary speech-makers and activists and their radical assemblies and political experiments were gone. And in the short run, their efforts had failed to make France a real democracy, like the one in the United States.

Yet the spirit and fundamental principles of the Revolution were far from dead. They survived and in the long run inspired the development of democratic societies not only in France but across the world. Indeed, says former Yale University scholar Robert R. Palmer, the Revolution "became lodged in the collective memory, a past event with which each succeeding generation had to come to terms. Some lived in fear, and others in hope, that the giant was only sleeping and might be aroused."[76]

The Sleeping Giant Awakes

The giant remained in relative slumber during the Napoléonic era, to be sure. After serving as First Consul for a few years, during which he dominated France's government, in 1804 Napoléon took the bold step of making himself emperor. He also pursued an extremely aggressive foreign policy. For several years his armies defeated those of other European nations, creating a vast French empire. But finally, in 1815, an alliance of British, Austrian, and Prussian forces beat Napoléon at Waterloo in Belgium, and he was exiled to an island in the south Atlantic.

After Napoléon's fall, the defeated French reinstated the monarchy. But they remembered the ideals of representative government that had emerged in the Revolution, so they placed certain constitutional limitations on royal power. Similarly, when King

Napoléon, and his wife, Josephine, being consecrated as emperor and empress of France by Pope Pius VII in 1804.

Louis-Philippe assumed the throne in 1830, he was forced to rule as a constitutional, rather than absolute, monarch. Even moderate monarchy proved unacceptable for many French, however. In 1848 they rose in a second revolution, dethroned Louis-Philippe, and established their Second Republic.

During this new upheaval, France's sleeping giant woke up. The original *Declaration of Rights* created by the revolutionaries of 1789 had not been forgotten and became a guiding force in shaping new laws and governmental institutions. The new constitution framed in 1848 provided for a democratic republic with a president, elected legislature, separation of powers, and universal voting rights.

The Global Spread of Popular Power

But it was not only France that had been indoctrinated with these democratic ideals. During the first few decades of the nineteenth century, they had spread outward and taken hold in various parts of Europe and beyond. A new spirit of resistance to oppression slowly but steadily grew into a sort of powder keg of revolutionary zeal. The 1848 uprising in France supplied the spark to ignite that keg. In that same year, revolutions exploded across the continent as the Austrians forced their king from his throne; the Hungarians demanded

The motto of the French Revolution, Liberty, Equality, and Fraternity, inspired other European nations to set up democratic governments.

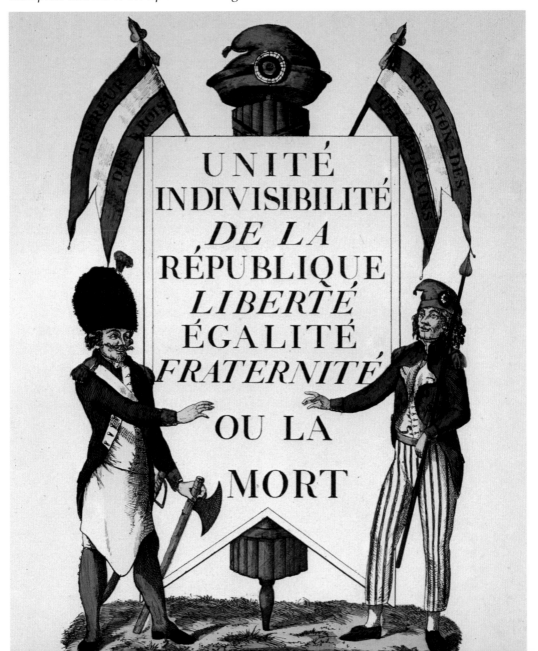

and won a new constitution that recognized human rights; and demands for democratic reforms arose in Germany, Italy, and elsewhere.

At this point, none of these nations completely abolished their old systems and set up open democracies. Yet they effectively planted the seeds that would later grow into the democratic Europe that emerged in the twentieth century. A kind of model or guiding force for change, the French Revolution had "introduced new crucial values, new status strivings, new levels of expectation," Palmer writes. "It changed the essence of the community and of the individual's sense of membership in it and his relationship to fellow citizens and fellow men. It even changed the feeling for history, or the idea of what could or ought to happen in history and in the world. . . . A whole system of civilization seemed to have fallen, and a new one to be struggling to be born."[77]

That struggle was also taking place in the Western Hemisphere. In Central and South America it was the French Revolution, not the American one, that served as the main inspiration and model for freedom fighters. This may be because these Latin American nations had originally been founded by Europeans; and they long retained strong cultural and political ties with Europe. In the 1800s, therefore, these peoples were well aware of the French Revolution and its democratic ideals. And over time they demanded and put them into practice. In this way scholar Anthony Arblaster states, France's grand political and social experiments in the 1790s

> transformed the modern history of democracy, [as] political ideas which had only been aspirations or dreams in the minds of [philosophers] and popular radicals, were placed on the agenda of real politics, not only in France or even Europe, but globally. The principles and example of the Revolution helped to inspire the first successful slave revolt in the Caribbean, in Haiti, as well as the political independence movements of South America. All such movements raised the issue of democracy, of popular power.[78]

Thus, by demonstrating that a country's people could dismantle its oppressive ancient order and rule themselves, the French Revolution helped to transform human civilization. The triumph of democracy in the modern world (with 123 nations having some form of democracy in 2006) owes an incalculable debt to the French. The waves they "set in motion in 1789," Palmer remarks, "have sometimes been stormy, sometimes more tranquil, but never quite calm—nor does it seem likely that they will ever wholly subside."[79]

Notes

Introduction: The Cradle of the Modern World

1. William Doyle, *The Oxford History of the French Revolution*. Oxford, England: Clarendon, 2002, pp. 424–25.

2. Jacques Solé, *Questions of the French Revolution: A Historical Overview*, trans. Shelley Temchin. New York: Pantheon, 1990, p. 236.

3. Doyle, *Oxford History*, p. 423.

Chapter 1: The Revolution's Complex Roots

4. William Doyle, *The French Revolution: A Very Short Introduction*. New York: Oxford University Press, 2001, p. 19.

5. Arthur J. May, *A History of Civilization: The Mid-Seventeenth Century to Modern Times*. New York: Scribners, 1964, p. 198.

6. Quoted in William Doyle, *Origins of the French Revolution*. Oxford, England: Oxford University Press, 1999, p. 51.

7. Doyle, *The French Revolution: A Very Short Introduction*, p. 21.

8. May, *A History of Civilization*, pp. 192, 196.

9. Quoted in Doyle, *The Oxford History of the French Revolution*, p. 38.

10. May, *A History of Civilization*, p. 197.

11. George Rudé, *The French Revolution: Its Causes, Its History, and Its Legacy After 200 Years*. New York: Weidenfeld and Nicolson, 1994, pp. 1–2.

12. John H. Stewart, ed., *A Documentary Survey of the French Revolution*. New York: Macmillan, 1971, pp. 12–13.

Chapter 2: Emergence of the National Assembly

13. Quoted in Laura Mason and Tracey Rizzo, *The French Revolution: A Document Collection*. Boston: Houghton Mifflin, 1999, p. 50.

14. R.K. Gooch, *Parliamentary Government in France: Revolutionary Origins, 1789–1791*. New York: Russell and Russell, 1971, p. 15.

15. Quoted in "Arthur Young's Travels in France During the Years 1787, 1788, 1789," Liberty Fund, Inc. (http://oll.libertyfund.org/title/292/7369).

16. Christopher Hibbert, *The Days of the French Revolution*. New York: HarperCollins, 1999, p. 49.

17. Quoted in Donald I. Wright, ed., *The French Revolution: Introductory Documents*. St. Lucia, Queensland: University of Queensland Press, 1994, pp. 31–32.

18. Quoted in Mason and Rizzo, *The French Revolution*, p. 58.

19. Quoted in Wright, *The French Revolution*, pp. 2–3.

20. Quoted in Hibbert, *The Days of the French Revolution*, pp. 53–54.

21. Leo Gershoy, *The French Revolution and Napoléon*. New York: Appleton-Century-Crofts, 1964, p. 109.

22. Quoted in Mason and Rizzo, *The French Revolution*, p. 59.

23. Quoted in Mason and Rizzo, *The French Revolution*, p. 61.

Chapter 3: The Revolution Turns Violent

24. Quoted in Mason and Rizzo, *The French Revolution*, pp. 61–62.

25. Quoted in Mason and Rizzo, *The French Revolution*, p. 64.

26. Quoted in Mason and Rizzo, *The French Revolution*, p. 65.

27. Quoted in Hibbert, *The Days of the French Revolution*, p. 62.

28. Quoted in Hibbert, *The Days of the French Revolution*, pp. 63–64.

29. Quoted in Georges Pernoud and Sabine Flaissier, eds., *The French Revolution*, trans. Richard Graves. New York: Capricorn, 1970, pp. 29–31.

30. Quoted in "A Defender of the Bastille Explains His Role," Liberty, Equality, Fraternity: Exploring the French Revolution (http://chnm.gmu.edu/revolution/d/383/).

31. Doyle, *The Oxford History of the French Revolution*, pp. 110–11.

32. Doyle, *The Oxford History of the French Revolution*, p. 115.

33. Quoted in Stewart, *A Documentary Survey of the French Revolution*, p. 107.

Chapter 4: A Constitution Forged in Blood

34. Quoted in Lynn Hunt, ed., *The French Revolution and Human Rights: A Brief Documentary History*. Boston: St. Martin's, 1996, p. 15.

35. Quoted in Frank Maloy Anderson, ed., *The Constitutions and Other Select Documents Illustrative of the History of France, 1789–1907*. New York: Russell and Russell, 1967, pp. 59–60.

36. Quoted in Mason and Rizzo, *The French Revolution*, p. 104.

37. Hunt, *The French Revolution and Human Rights*, p. 15.

38. Quoted in Earl Leroy Higgins, ed., *The French Revolution as Told by Contemporaries*. Boston: Houghton Mifflin, 1980, p. 130.

39. Quoted in Hunt, *The French Revolution and Human Rights*, pp. 93–94.

40. Mason and Rizzo, *The French Revolution*, p. 93.

41. Quoted in "The September Massacres," Liberty, Equality, Fraternity: Exploring the French Revolution (http://chnm.gmu.edu/revolution/d/392/).

42. Norah Lofts and Margery Weiner, *Eternal France: A History of France from the French Revolution Through World War II*. London: Curtis Brown, 1968, p. 19.

43. Lofts and Weiner, *Eternal France,* pp. 19–20.

Chapter 5: Terror in the Name of Liberty

44. Quoted in Mason and Rizzo, *The French Revolution*, pp. 255–57.

45. Quoted in Stewart, *A Documentary Survey of the French Revolution*, p. 472.

46. R.F. Leslie, *The Age of Transformation, 1789 to 1871*. New York: Harper and Row, 1967, p. 50.

47. Quoted in Higgins, *The French Revolution as Told by Contemporaries*, p. 307.

48. Quoted in Wright, *The French Revolution*, pp. 154–55.

49. Quoted in Stewart, *A Documentary Survey of the French Revolution*, p. 478.

50. Quoted in Anderson, *The Constitutions and Other Selected Documents*, pp. 154–56.

51. Hibbert, *The Days of the French Revolution*, pp. 226–27.

52. Quoted in Hibbert, *The Days of the French Revolution*, p. 222.

53. Quoted in Henry Morse Stephens, *The Principal Speeches of the Statesmen and Orators of the French Revolution, 1789–1795*, vol. 2. Oxford, England: Clarendon, 1892, p. 275.

54. Quoted in John Paxton, *Companion to the French Revolution*. New York: Facts on File, 1989, p. 166.

55. Quoted in Higgins, *The French Revolution as Told by Contemporaries*, p. 357.

Chapter 6: Changes in French Society and Culture

56. Emmet Kennedy, *A Cultural History of the French Revolution*. New Haven: Yale University Press, 1991, p. 145.

57. Quoted in Mason and Rizzo, *The French Revolution*, p. 104.

58. Quoted in Kennedy, *A Cultural History of the French Revolution*, p. 150.

59. Hibbert, *The Days of the French Revolution*, pp. 231–33.

60. Quoted in "Religion: The Cult of the Supreme Being," Liberty, Equality, Fraternity: Exploring the French Revolution (http://chnm.gmu.edu/revolution/d/436/).

61. Quoted in Stewart, *A Documentary Survey of the French Revolution*, pp. 369–70.

62. Quoted in "Primary Schools," Liberty, Equality, Fraternity: Exploring the French Revolution (http://chnm.gmu.edu/revolution/d/464/).

63. Quoted in Doyle, *Oxford History*, pp. 420–21.

64. Olwen Hufton, "Voilà la Citoyenne," in *History Today*, May 1989, pp. 27–28.

65. Quoted in Olympe de Gouges, "The Declaration of Rights of Woman," Liberty, Equality, Fraternity: Exploring the French Revolution (http://chnm.gmu.edu/revolution/d/293/).

66. Lynn Hunt, "The Unstable Boundaries of the French Revolution," in Philippe Ariès and Georges Duby, eds., *A History of Private Life*, vol. 4.,

trans. by Arthur Goldhammer. *From the Fires of Revolution to the Great War*. ed. Michelle Perrot. Cambridge, MA: Harvard University Press, 1990, p. 30.

Chapter 7: Napoléon and the Revolution's End

67. Quoted in "Dismantling the Terror: Parliamentarianism Reasserted," Liberty, Equality, Fraternity: Exploring the French Revolution (http://chnm.gmu.edu/revolution/d/448/).

68. Quoted in "Constitution of the Year III (1795)," Liberty, Equality, Fraternity: Exploring the French Revolution (http://chnm.gmu.edu/revolution/d/430/).

69. Donald Kagan, Steven Ozment, and Frank M. Turner, *The Western Heritage*. New York: Prentice-Hall, 2006, p. 672.

70. Hibbert, *The Days of the French Revolution*, p. 295.

71. Martyn Lyons, *Napoléon Bonaparte and the Legacy of the French Revolution*.

New York: St. Martin's Press, 1994, p. 16.

72. Quoted in "Napoléon's Proclamation to His Troops in Italy (March–April 1796)," The History Guide (www.historyguide.org/intellect/nap1796.html).

73. Lyons, *Napoléon Bonaparte*, p. 15.

74. Lyons, *Napoléon Bonaparte*, pp. 24–25.

75. Quoted in Stewart, *A Documentary Survey of the French Revolution*, p. 780.

Epilogue: The Revolution's Formidable Legacy

76. Robert R. Palmer, *The World of the French Revolution*. New York: Harper-Collins, 1972, p. 251.

77. Palmer, *The World of the French Revolution*, p. 441.

78. Anthony Arblaster, *Democracy*. Philadelphia: Open University Press, 2002, p. 38.

79. Palmer, *The World of the French Revolution*, p. 270.

For Further Reading

Books

Olivier Bernier, *Words of Fire, Deeds of Blood: The Mob, the Monarchy, and the French Revolution*. Boston: Little, Brown, 1992. One of the better modern overviews of the subject.

Thomas Carlyle, *The French Revolution: A History*. New York: Modern Library, 2002. First published in 1837, this classic overview of the Revolution is written in an exuberant, emotional style that resembles epic poetry. Still valuable but should be used to supplement more up-to-date histories, such as Doyle's and Hibbert's (see below) rather than by itself.

William Doyle, *Origins of the French Revolution*. Oxford, England: Oxford University Press, 1999. Considered by many experts to be the most insightful synopsis of the Revolution's causes.

William Doyle, *The Oxford History of the French Revolution*. Oxford, England: Clarendon, 2002. One of the two or three most comprehensive and reliable existing overviews of the Revolution. Highly recommended.

Will and Ariel Durant, *Rousseau and Revolution*. New York: MJF Books, 1997. This Pulitzer Prize–winning work by the late, great historian Will Durant remains an astonishingly comprehensive, well-documented, engrossing,

and valuable study of the philosophical roots of the Revolution. A must for French Revolution buffs.

Christopher Hibbert, *The Days of the French Revolution*. New York: HarperCollins, 1999. An excellent recent treatment of the Revolution.

Emmet Kennedy, *A Cultural History of the French Revolution*. New Haven: Yale University Press, 1991. One of the better studies of religion, education, art, music, theater, and other aspects of French culture during the Revolution.

Laura Mason and Tracey Rizzo, *The French Revolution: A Document Collection*. Boston: Houghton Mifflin, 1999. A useful collection of primary source documents about the Revolution.

George Rudé, *The French Revolution: Its Causes, Its History, and Its Legacy After 200 Years*. New York: Weidenfeld and Nicolson, 1994. Does a good job of describing the Revolution and placing it in a larger historical context via its legacy.

Simon Schama, *Citizens: A Chronicle of the French Revolution*. New York: Knopf, 2005. A large, sprawling treatment of the subject with a controversial and somewhat flawed slant—that the Revolution was driven more by the self-delusion and violent acts of a few leaders than by the French people and their strivings for liberty—but still valuable for its detailed, often arresting descriptions of various events.

Internet

The Execution of Louis XVI, 1793, Eyewitness to History (http://www.eye witnesstohistory.com/louis.htm). A useful brief description of the last days of the French king whose reign ended in tragedy and helped spark the French Revolution.

French Revolution. Microsoft Encarta Online Encyclopedia (http://encarta. msn.com/encyclopedia_761557826/ French_Revolution.html). A fine brief overview of the Revolution by MSN/Encarta.

Liberty, Equality, Fraternity: Exploring the French Revolution. George Mason University and City University of New York (chnm.gmu. edu/revolution). This collaboration of scholars from George Mason University and the City University of New York is possibly the best general site about the Revolution on the Internet. In addition to historical overviews, it contains hundreds of primary source documents pertaining to the Revolution. Highly recommended.

Tom Holberg, **Napoléon and the French Revolution,** Napoléon Bonaparte Internet Guide (www.napo leonbonaparte.nl/html/body_nap_ and_revolution.html). A good overview of Napoléon's role in the Revolution, with links to other useful sites about Napoléon and what he did in the Revolution's aftermath.

Index

execution of, 64
  Mountain and, 51
de-Christianization, 69–71
Declaration of Independence (American),
  44, 46
Declaration of Rights of Women, The
  (Gouges), 75
Declaration of the Rights of Man and of the
  Citizen, 44, 45, 69, 90
"Defense of the Republic Levy," 58–59
Desmoulins, Camille, 64
Diderot, Denis, 75
Directory
  establishment of, 80
  members of, 80
  Napoleon and, 83, 84–85, 86
  overthrow of, 86–87
  war waged by, 81–82
divorce, 77
Doyle, William
  on acceptance by Louis XVI of end of
    power, 41
  on *cahiers de doléances*, 28
  on effect of French Revolution, 8, 11
  on French Revolution as series of devel-
    opments, 12
draft (military), 58–59
Duran-Maillane, Pierre-Toussaint, 78

education, 66, 71–73
Egypt, 85
émigrés, 49, 51
Encyclopedia, The (Diderot), 75
enemies of Revolution, 60–62
Enlightenment, 20–22, 71
Estates General
  call for meeting of, 23–24
  credentials of delegates and voting in,
    29
  described, 23
  Louis XVI and, 23–25, 26
  See also National Assembly
executions
  of innocent people, 62
  of Louis XVI, 53–54, 57

of Marie-Antoinette, 63
number of, 57
of political leaders, 64–65
use of guillotine for, 56

feudal system, 18, 42, 43
First Coalition, 57, 58
First Estate. *See* nobility
France
  population of, 12
  power of, 10–11, 12–13
  Seven Years War and, 13–14
French Revolution
  change in political system and, 8–10
  end of, 87–88
  in France after Napoleon, 89–90
  as model for other nations, 11, 91–92
  as series of developments, 12
French soldiers
  Revolutionary Army, 82–83
  royal, 31, 37–38

Germany, 92
Gershoy, Leo, 30
Girodins
  control of Legislative Assembly by, 51
  described, 50
  execution of Louis XVI and, 54
  murder of Marat and, 59
Gooch, R.K., 25
Gouges, Olympe de, 75
Gouze, Marie, 75
governments
  constitutional monarchies, 33, 48, 89–90
  Consulate, 85–87, 89
  Convention
    Committee of Public Safety and, 60
    creation of, 53
    declarations of war by, 51, 57
    educational reforms of, 72–73
    end of Terror and, 78–79
    problems faced by, 55
  Directory, 80–83, 84–85, 86
  ideas of Montesquieu about, 21
  Legislative Assembly, 50–51

Picture Credits

Cover: © North Wind Picture Archives
AFP/Getty Images, 56
AP Images, 45
The Art Archive/Alfredo Dagli Orti/Musee Carnavalet Paris/The Picture Desk, Inc., 19
The Art Archive/Gianni Dagli Orti/Bibliotheque des Arts Decoratifs Paris/The Picture Desk, Inc., 7 (lower left), 38
The Art Archive/Gianni Dagli Orti/Fondation Thiers Paris/The Picture Desk, Inc., 84
The Art Archive/Gianni Dagli Orti/Musee Carnavalet Paris/The Picture Desk, Inc., 6 (upper), 6 (lower left), 10, 18 (right), 47, 50, 62, 70
The Art Archive/Gianni Dagli Orti/Musee du Chateau de Versailles/The Picture Desk, Inc., 71, 76
The Art Archive/Gianni Dagli Orti/Museo del Risorgimento Rome/The Picture Desk, Inc., 7 (lower right)
The Art Archive/Gianni Dagli Orti/Napoleonic Museum Rome/The Picture Desk, Inc., 90

The Art Archive/Marc Charmet/Bibliotheque Nationale Paris/The Picture Desk, Inc., 42
The Art Archive/Marc Charmet/The Picture Desk, Inc., 9, 24, 39, 52, 61, 74
The Art Archive/The Picture Desk, Inc., 25, 68, 79, 91
©Bibliotheque Nationale, Paris, France/Lauros/Giraudon/The Bridgeman Art Library, 82
The Bridgeman Art Library/Getty Images, 6 (lower right)
Eileen Tweedy/General Wolfe Museum Quebec House/The Art Archive, 14
©Fogg Art Museum, Harvard University Art Museums, USA/Bequest of Grenville L. Wintrop/The Bridgeman Art Library, 27
Hulton Archive/Getty Images, 34, 35, 57
Kean Collection/Hulton Archive/Getty Images, 15
©Musee de la Ville de Paris, Musee Carnavalet, Paris, France/The Bridgeman Art Library, 30
Roger Viollet/Getty Images, 18 (left)
Stock Montage/Hulton Archive/Getty Images, 20
Time & Life Pictures/Getty Images, 86

About the Author

In addition to his acclaimed volumes on the ancient world, historian Don Nardo has written and edited many books for young adults about modern history and government, including *The Mexican-American War, The Declaration of Independence, The Bill of Rights, The Age of Colonialism, The Great Depression,* and *World War II in the Pacific.* Mr. Nardo also writes screenplays and teleplays and composes music. He lives with his wife, Christine, in Massachusetts.

Property of
Bradley Beach Public Library